FOR EVERY SEASON

There is a Salad

LINDA STEIDEL

FOR EVERY SEASON THERE IS A SALAD

Copyright © 2010

Library of Congress Control Number: 2009940236
ISBN: 978-0-9819290-5-7

Author: Linda Steidel

Publishing Agent: Brio Press
12 South Sixth Street #1250
Minneapolis, Minnesota 55402

Photography: Mark Choate
Cover Design and Layout: Anthony Sclavi

I am profoundly grateful for the constant support of my students and friends. I love teaching, and they inspire me to excel. Their loyalty keeps me on my toes and I want them to continue to be there for me. They make my job "and I really can't call it a job" so much fun. I am sure that I am the one who learns the most at any given class.

There are really no words that can adequately say "thank you" to my partner, friend, designer and photographer, Mark Choate. He understood from the very beginning what I hoped to accomplish and share with you. His photos are magic and, although he claims to never be able to eat salad again, he captured the essence of these recipes in his pictures. It was very important to me that all of the pictures be real photos of the salads that I re-created and he photographed. His wife, Cindy, and our friends ate their way through every single salad in the book. All of the photos were taken in my home, Mark and Cindy's home, or local farmers' markets. They are beautiful. As these projects evolve, more and more people become invaluable in the process. A good idea can only come to fruition with the help of many. I would like to thank the entire team at Brio Press. Will, Anthony (our artist!) and Sadie "got" it and the concept that Mark and I wanted for the book. Thank you so very much for your vision and creativity.

I am continually inspired by favorite chefs, great restaurants and international culture. My extensive travels have allowed me to experience the amazing food of each country and region, and to learn cooking techniques from the wonderful local people.

Thank you one and all. I am so grateful for this opportunity.

Linda

Growing up in Texas I must say salad played a very small role. Barbecue, huge . . . salad, not so much. A little iceberg lettuce with some tomato and any bottled dressing on hand did it for the salad.

Since I started teaching cooking classes, salad became my biggest challenge. There are so many exciting ingredients that can go into one. It never has to be boring. Salad evolves by combining many flavors. Salty, creamy, cool, fresh.

Add to that different cheeses, nuts, toasted seeds and vegetables or fish (cooked, smoked or canned), shellfish, meat, pork or grilled chicken. These salads become a complete meal. Other layers such as cured meats, like prosciutto, salami or soppresata and fresh fruit change the ordinary into the spectacular.

Dressing the salad is primary and should enhance all of the ingredients. Look for a contrast of salty and sweet, crunchy and smooth, bitter and smoky.

The quality of the ingredients is key. Always buy fresh, colorful, and in season. Every dish will be healthy, fresh and satisfying. Salad can reach new heights by using a little imagination, checking out your local farmers market and experimenting.

Just a salad? . . .
Never!

Have fun and enjoy
FOR EVERY SEASON
There is a Salad

Summer

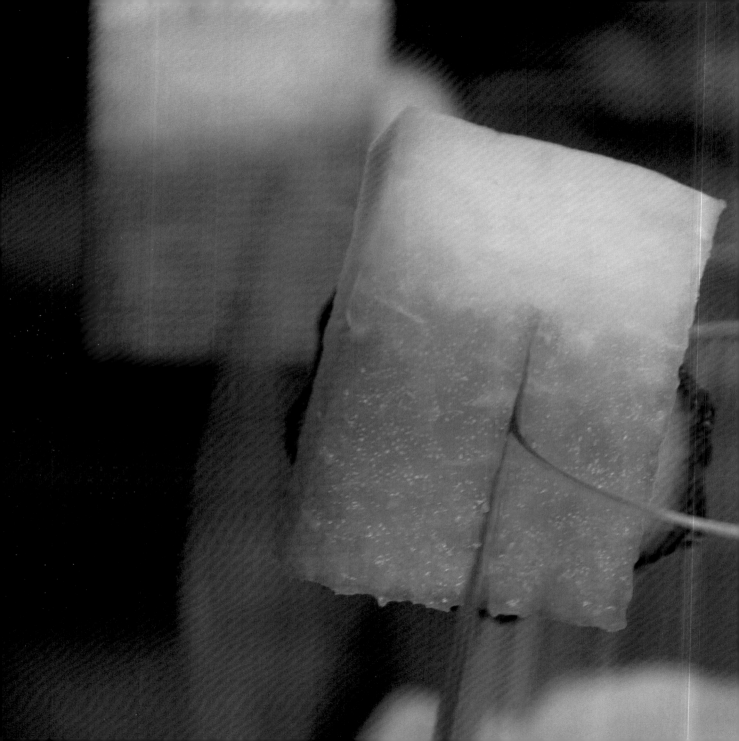

Summer

Autumn

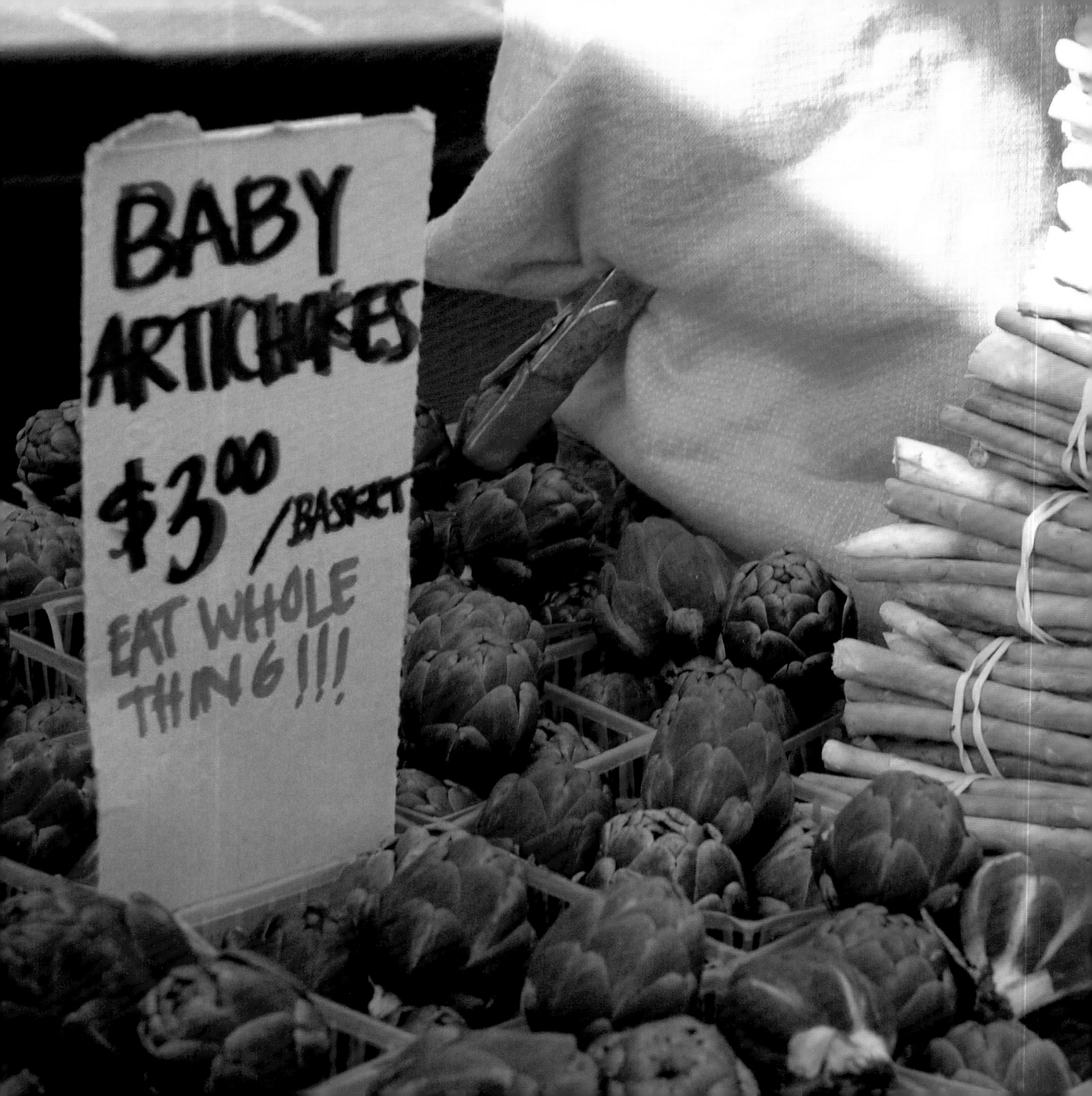
BABY
ARTICHOKES
$3.00 /BASKET
EAT WHOLE
THING!!!

Autumn

Winter

Winter

Spring

Spring

Dressings & Accoutrements

summer

Grilled Hot Dog Potato Salad

3 medium russet potatoes
(about 2 1/2 pounds)
1/4 cup olive oil
1 pound good quality hot dogs, pierced
1/4 cup chopped fresh
Italian parsley leaves
2 tablespoons chopped fresh basil leaves
Salt and freshly ground black pepper

Boil the potatoes until tender, about 10 minutes. Drain and cool to room temperature. Peel the potatoes and cut into bite size pieces.

Put the hot dogs onto a hot grill pan and cook until golden brown, about 10 minutes. Cool the hot dogs to room temperature, then cut them crosswise into bite size pieces.

Toss the potatoes, parsley, basil and olive oil in a large bowl. Season the potato salad with salt and pepper to taste. Add the hot dogs to the salad and toss. Season to taste, adding additional olive oil if needed. Serve the salad at room temperature.

Serves 6

Kids big and small love this.
Charred hot dogs add to the perfect summer barbecue.

PASTRY

1 3/4 cups all-purpose flour
1/2 teaspoon sugar
1/2 teaspoon salt
1 stick cold unsalted butter, cut into pieces
1 large egg, lightly beaten

If making pastry makes you crazy, buy store made or use puff pastry. Both are great.

FILLING

1 cup milk
3/4 cup freshly grated Parmigiano-Reggiano cheese (4 ounces)
1 cup heavy cream
3 large eggs, lightly beaten
1/2 teaspoon salt

TOMATO CONFIT

2 pounds plum tomatoes, peeled, quartered and seeded
24 small thyme sprigs
3 garlic cloves, thinly sliced
2 tablespoons olive oil
Salt and freshly ground pepper

Parmesan Tartlets with Tomato Confit & Baby Lettuces

For the pastry: In a food processor, combine the flour with the sugar and salt. Add the butter and pulse until the mixture resembles coarse meal. Beat the egg with the water and pour it into the food processor. Pulse several times until the pastry is moist and forms into a ball. Divide the dough into 8 equal pieces. Flatten each piece into a 3-inch disk, wrap in plastic and refrigerate for a few minutes.

Preheat the oven to 350 degrees. On a lightly floured surface, roll out the pastry into a 6-inch round. Fit it into a 4-inch fluted tartlet pan with a removable bottom; cut off any overhang. Lightly prick the bottom with a fork. Repeat with the remaining pastry. Set the pans on a baking sheet and bake for 30 minutes, or until the pastry is golden and cooked through.

Make the filling: In a food processor, blend the milk with the cheese until smooth. Add the cream, eggs and salt and pulse just until combined. Pour the mixture into the tartlet shells and bake for 15 minutes, or until the custard is just set. Let cool for 10 minutes, then unmold the tartlets. Serve hot or at room temperature with the Tomato Confit.

For the Confit: Preheat the oven to 350 degrees and line a rimmed baking sheet with parchment paper. Arrange the tomatoes on the sheet, rounded sides down, and top with the thyme, garlic and olive oil. Season with salt and pepper. Roast the tomatoes for 50 minutes to 1 hour, or until they are softened and the garlic is golden.

Serve the tartlets with baby lettuces that have been lightly dressed with olive oil and lemon juice.

Serves 8

Hearts of Romaine, Watercress & Avocado Salad with Jalapeño-Lime Vinaigrette

1 package hearts of romaine
2 cups organic watercress
2 avocados, pitted and peeled
3 tablespoons toasted pumpkin seeds

VINAIGRETTE
2 tablespoons sugar
1/4 cup freshly squeezed lime juice
2 red or green jalapeño chiles, stemmed, seeded, and minced
1/4 teaspoon salt
1/4 teaspoon freshly ground black pepper
3 shallots, minced
1/4 teaspoon toasted ground cumin seeds
1 1/2 cups olive oil

To make the vinaigrette, combine the sugar and lime juice, and mix until the sugar dissolves. Add the jalapeño, salt, pepper, shallots and cumin; whisk until the salt dissolves. In a slow steady stream, whisk in the olive oil until the dressing is well emulsified.

Cut the romaine hearts into quarters lengthwise and put them in a large bowl. Trim off the roots of the watercress.

To serve, gently toss the romaine with enough dressing to coat. Cross 2 wedges of romaine on each plate. Using the same bowl, toss the watercress with a little more of the dressing, and sprinkle some watercress over the romaine. Cut each half avocado into 6 lengthwise slices. Arrange 3 slices of avocado over each salad, then finish with a sprinkling of pumpkin seeds and a drizzle of additional dressing.

Serves 6

Garden Greens with
Lime-Basil Dressing & Tear Drop Tomatoes

6 large portions of salad greens
1 box of tear drop tomatoes

LIME-BASIL DRESSING
1/3 cup fresh basil leaves,
packed tightly
2 limes, juice of 2, zest of 1
1 cup heavy cream
3 tablespoons honey
1/3 cup champagne vinegar
1 tablespoon shallots, diced
1 teaspoon garlic, minced
3/4 teaspoon salt

Place the basil, lime zest and juice in a blender. Add the remainder of the ingredients and blend until smooth.

Place the salad and tomatoes in a large bowl. Add enough dressing to lightly coat all of the leaves.

Serves 6

I love adding honey to vinaigrettes. It gives them a very smooth, finished flavor.

Greek Orzo & Grilled Shrimp Salad with Mustard-Dill Vinaigrette

1 pound orzo, cooked al dente
1 large cucumber, seeded, quartered lengthwise and sliced
4 green onions, thinly sliced
1 pint grape tomatoes, halved
1 cup sliced Kalamata olives
1/4 cup chopped fresh dill
1/4 cup white wine vinegar
3 tablespoons Dijon mustard
1/2 cup olive oil, plus additional for brushing shrimp
Salt and freshly ground pepper
3/4 pound feta cheese, crumbled
16 medium shrimp, peeled and de-veined

Combine orzo, cucumber, green onions, tomatoes and olives in a large bowl.

Place dill, vinegar and mustard in a blender and blend until smooth. With the motor running, slowly add the olive oil and blend until emulsified. Season with salt and pepper to taste.

Pour the vinaigrette over the orzo mixture and stir well to combine.

Gently fold in the feta cheese. Heat grill to high. Brush shrimp with oil and season with salt and pepper. Grill for approximately 2 minutes per side or until just cooked through. Divide orzo salad among plates and top with shrimp. Garnish with additional dill.

Serve with grilled flatbread.

Serve 6

This salad is also great with grilled sea scallops, salmon or halibut. Perfect for summer.

Shaved Summer Squash, Arugula & Pine Nut Salad

1 small green summer squash or zucchini
1 small yellow summer squash
6 ounces arugula
1/4 cup olive oil
1 tablespoon lemon juice
1 tablespoon chopped mint
1/4 cup pine nuts, toasted
Salt and pepper to taste
Parmigiano-Reggiano cheese

Using a vegetable slicer or mandolin, slice squash length-wise into thin strips.

Combine with the arugula, olive oil, lemon juice, mint and pine nuts in a stainless steel bowl. Season with salt and pepper and toss to evenly distribute.

Garnish with shavings of cheese and serve.

NOTE: Toast the pine nuts in a dry non-stick skillet until golden.

Serves 6

Mint gives this salad a really fresh, clean taste.

Grilled Apple, Arugula & Blue Cheese Salad

3 Granny Smith apples, halved and cored
3 slices crusty Tuscan bread,
cut into 1-inch chunks
2 bunches arugula, trimmed and
torn into large pieces
1 cup seedless red grapes, halved
1/2 cup olive oil
1/4 cup red wine vinegar
Salt and freshly ground pepper to taste
1/3 cup crumbled blue cheese

Grilling the apples caramelizes the cut sides and brings the sugar to the surface.

Place the apples cut-side down on the grill over a medium-hot grill and cook for about 5 minutes, or until well browned. At the same time, place the bread on the grill and toast until golden brown. Remove the apples and bread from the grill as they are done.

When they are cool enough to handle, cut the apples into thin slices and toss in a bowl with the bread.

Add the arugula, grapes, olive oil, vinegar, and salt and pepper to taste and toss well. Just before serving, sprinkle with the blue cheese.

Serves 6

Country-Style Greek Salad

6 heirloom tomatoes, cored
and cut into wedges
4 garlic cloves, minced
Sea salt
Freshly ground black pepper
1 small red onion, peeled and
cut in half lengthwise
3 cucumbers, peeled, halved and seeded
2 roasted peppers, from a jar
1/2 cup minced fresh Italian parsley
8 ounces feta cheese, crumbled
1 tablespoon capers, rinsed
1/3 cup fruity olive oil
2 tablespoons red wine vinegar
Juice of 1 lemon
1/2 cup Kalamata olives
2 tablespoons fresh oregano leaves
1/2 teaspoon sea salt
Country-style bread, cut into thick slices

Arrange the tomatoes in a wide, shallow bowl, scatter the garlic on top, season with salt and pepper, and set aside for 30 minutes.

Cut both onion halves into very thin, crosswise slices and scatter them over the tomatoes. Cut the cucumbers crosswise into thick half-moons, add them, along with the roasted pepper strips, to the tomatoes and onions, and toss very gently.

Top the vegetables with the parsley, feta and capers, drizzle the olive oil on top, and sprinkle the vinegar and lemon juice over everything. Add the olives, sprinkle with oregano and sea salt. Serve with country-style bread.

Serves 6

This salad is served every day in Greece for lunch or dinner. The secret is using a very creamy, non-salty feta cheese.

Fresh Mozzarella Salad with Avocado, Roasted Corn & Grape Tomatoes

4 ears sweet corn, in the husk
1/2 pound fresh mozzarella,
cut into 1/4-inch cubes
2 ripe avocados, halved,
peeled and cut into 1/4-inch cubes
1/2 pint grape or
other small tomato varieties, halved
8 to 10 fresh basil leaves,
cut into thin strips
Sea salt and freshly ground
black pepper to taste
1/2 cup Herb Vinaigrette
(see next page)
Baby greens or arugula

Preheat the oven to 400 degrees.

Soak the corn in the sink for 10 to 15 minutes. Place on a baking sheet with sides and roast for 20 to 25 minutes, until the kernels are tender. Cool to room temperature, then pull off and discard the husks and silks. Cut the kernels off the cob into a large bowl.

Add the mozzarella, avocados, tomatoes, basil, salt and pepper to the bowl with the corn. Drizzle 1/2 cup of the vinaigrette over the salad and toss gently. Be careful not to over-mix or mash the avocado. Season with more salt, pepper or vinaigrette to taste. Serve on a bed of arugula or baby greens.

Serves 6

The corn can also be grilled. If you have the barbecue on, add some chicken with barbecue sauce for a great summer supper.

Herb Vinaigrette

1/3 cup red wine vinegar
2 teaspoons Dijon mustard
Grated zest and juice of 1 lemon
2 or 3 fresh basil leaves,
cut into thin strips
2 tablespoons chopped
fresh oregano leaves
2 tablespoons chopped
fresh flat-leaf parsley leaves
3/4 cup olive oil
Sea salt and freshly ground
black pepper to taste

Combine the vinegar, mustard, lemon zest, juice, basil, oregano and parsley in a small bowl and stir to mix. Whisk in the olive oil in a slow steady stream until all of the oil is incorporated. Season with salt and pepper. Use immediately or store refrigerated in an airtight container for up to 3 days.

Deviled Egg-Stuffed Avocados on Lime Slaw

8 large eggs
2 tablespoons pickle relish
2 tablespoons mayonnaise
1 tablespoon seeded and
chopped jalapeño
1 medium rib celery, diced
2 tablespoons roughly chopped
fresh cilantro
Salt and freshly ground
black pepper to taste
3 avocados, peeled,
pitted and diced medium, save the shells
1/4 cup vegetable oil
8 flour or corn tortillas

SLAW
2 cups thinly sliced red cabbage
1/4 cup olive oil
1/4 cup fresh lime juice
1/4 cup molasses
1/4 cup red wine vinegar
Salt and pepper to taste

The deviled egg mixture is also great if you add some cooked shrimp or crab.

Place the eggs in a saucepan and cover with cold water. Bring the water to a boil, reduce the heat to low and simmer for 10 minutes. Drain and run under cold water to stop the cooking.

Peel the eggs and place them in a medium bowl. Add the relish, mayonnaise, jalapeno, celery, cilantro and salt and pepper to taste and mash together with a fork, until the mixture is pretty uniform. Gently fold in the chopped avocado. Stuff one quarter of the mixture into the center of each avocado shell and set aside.

In a large saute pan, heat the vegetable oil until hot but not smoking. Place a tortilla in the pan and fry, turning once, until just crisp and lightly browned, 1 to 2 minutes. Remove to paper towels to drain and repeat with remaining tortillas. Break the tortillas into chips.

Make the slaw: In a large bowl, combine all the ingredients and mix well. Place the slaw on individual serving plates, top with the stuffed avocado halves, and serve, passing the tortilla chips separately.

Serves 6

Grilling the pita bread makes it very crispy. Sometimes instead of tearing the bread I leave it whole and serve the salad on top. Add some grilled swordfish for a delicious main course.

Grilled Zucchini & Bell Pepper Fattoush

GRILL

3 medium red & orange bell peppers,
stemmed, seeded and quartered
4 to 5 slender zucchini, trimmed, cut
lengthwise in half
2, 5 to 6-inch pita breads,
each cut horizontally into 2 disks
Olive oil

1 8-ounce cucumber, peeled, halved,
seeded, cut into 1/2-inch cubes
12 cherry tomatoes, each halved
3 green onions, thinly sliced
1 cup pitted Kalamata olives, halved
1/2 cup fresh mint leaves
1/3 cup chopped fresh cilantro
1/2 cup olive oil
1/4 cup fresh lemon juice
1 teaspoon ground cumin
1 4-ounce piece feta cheese,
cut into 1/2-inch cubes

Prepare barbecue. Brush peppers, zucchini and bread on both sides with oil. Sprinkle lightly with salt and pepper. Grill peppers and zucchini until lightly charred and just tender, turning often, about 6 minutes. Transfer vegetables to a foil-lined baking sheet. Grill bread until lightly charred and just crisp, turning often, about 3 minutes. Transfer to sheet with vegetables and cool. Tear bread into 1-inch pieces.

Cut peppers lengthwise into 1/2-inch wide strips, then crosswise into 1/2-inch pieces. Cut zucchini lengthwise in half, then crosswise into 1/2-inch pieces. Place in a large bowl.

Add cucumber, tomatoes, green onions, olives, mint and cilantro and toss to combine. Add bread pieces. Whisk 1/2 cup oil, lemon juice and cumin in small bowl to blend. Season dressing to taste with salt and pepper. Add dressing to salad; toss to coat. Add feta and gently mix into salad.

Transfer salad to large bowl or platter and serve.

Serves 6

Small seedless watermelons are great for this salad. For brunch or lunch this is a delicious dish. Just add some toasted naan to complete the flavors.

Curried Crab & Watermelon Salad with Arugula

3 tablespoons olive oil
2 tablespoons finely chopped Granny Smith apple
1 tablespoon finely chopped onion
1 1/2 teaspoons curry powder
Pinch of saffron threads, crumbled
1 teaspoon water
1/2 cup mayonnaise
1 tablespoon finely chopped cilantro
1 tablespoon finely chopped mint
Salt and freshly ground pepper
1 pound lump crabmeat
Six 1/2-inch-thick half-round watermelon slices from a large watermelon, rind removed
2 1/3 tablespoons fresh lime juice
2 bunches of arugula, large stems discarded

In a small saucepan, heat 1 tablespoon of the olive oil until shimmering. Add the apple, onion, curry and saffron and cook over moderate heat until the onion is softened, about 5 minutes. Remove from the heat and stir in the water; let cool.

Scrape the onion-curry mixture into a mini-processor. Add the mayonnaise and process until smooth. Transfer the curried mayonnaise to a medium bowl, add the cilantro and mint, and season with salt and pepper. Gently fold the crabmeat into the curried mayonnaise.

Cut each slice of watermelon into 2 triangles and transfer to plates. Season the watermelon with salt and pepper and sprinkle each serving with 1 teaspoon of lime juice. Mound the crab salad on the watermelon triangles.

In another bowl, toss the arugula with the remaining 1 tablespoon of lime juice and the remaining 2 tablespoons olive oil and season with salt and pepper. Arrange the dressed arugula on the plates and serve.

Serves 6

2 large ripe beefsteak or heirloom
tomatoes (about 1 pound),
cored and sliced 1/2 inch thick
1 teaspoon sea salt
1/2 teaspoon freshly ground black pepper
1/2 cup all-purpose flour
1/2 cup yellow cornmeal
2 tablespoons sugar
1 large egg

1/2 cup well-shaken buttermilk
Canola oil for frying (about 1/2 cup)
4 large green tomatoes,
cored and sliced 1/2 inch thick
1/2 pint grape or small heirloom tomatoes
(such as Sweet 100's), halved lengthwise
4 ounces goat cheese
8 fresh basil leaves, cut into thin strips
Sweet Basil Vinaigrette

Fried Heirloom Tomato & Sweet 100 Tomato Salad

Preheat the oven to 200 degrees. Line a baking sheet with paper towels.

Arrange the ripe tomato slices in one layer on a large platter or on individual plates. Season with salt and pepper to taste.

Stir the flour, cornmeal, sugar, 1 teaspoon salt and pepper in a small bowl.

Whisk the egg and buttermilk together in a separate small bowl.

Pour enough oil in a large skillet to fill to ¼ inch deep and heat over medium-high heat to about 375 degrees, or until the oil sizzles when you drop a small amount of flour into the skillet.

Dip a green tomato slice in the egg-buttermilk mixture to coat both sides, dredge it in the flour mixture to coat both sides, and place it in the hot oil. Repeat with enough tomato slices to fill the skillet without crowding and fry until the under sides are golden brown, about 2 minutes. Turn and fry the other side to golden brown. Use tongs or a slotted spatula to transfer the fried tomato slices to the prepared baking sheet to drain; place the sheet in the oven while you fry the remaining green tomatoes.

Arrange the fried tomato slices on top of the fresh tomato slices. Scatter the small tomatoes over the slices and sprinkle with the crumbled goat cheese. Drizzle with 1/2 cup of the vinaigrette and top with the basil strips (see recipe on page 184). Season with additional salt and pepper and add more vinaigrette to taste. Serve immediately.

Serves 6-8

Grilled Caprese Salad with Basil Oil

2 cups fresh basil leaves
1/2 cup olive oil, divided
1/3 cup white wine vinegar
3 tablespoons Parmesan, grated
Salt and pepper to taste
4 large tomatoes,
sliced horizontally into thirds
6 ounces fresh mozzarella, cut into 8
slices

Process basil, 1/3 cup oil, vinegar, Parmesan, salt and pepper in a food processor until smooth.

Coat tomato slices with remaining oil and season with salt and pepper. Grill tomatoes on 1 side for 1 minute, then flip (do not flip the tops). Arrange cheese on tomato slices and grill until it begins to melt, 1 to 2 minutes.

Assemble stacks with 2 cheese topped slices and 1 top. Serve with basil sauce.

Serves 4

Great presentation!

Tomato and Onion Tart

Serve this tart with a simple green salad for a beautiful luncheon entrée.

2 large onions
(about 1 1/2 pounds) sliced thin
2 tablespoons olive oil
1/2 pound dry Jack or Gruyère cheese,
shredded (about 2 cups)
1/2 pound plum tomatoes
cut into 1/2-inch wedges
1/2 pound medium yellow tomatoes or 1/2
pound plum tomatoes
cut into 1/2-inch wedges
1/4 cup Niçoise olives, pitted
One recipe for butter pastry dough

BUTTER PASTRY DOUGH
2 cups all-purpose flour
1 1/2 teaspoons salt
1 1/2 sticks cold unsalted butter,
cut into bits
6 - 7 tablespoons ice water

In a large heavy skillet cook onions with salt to taste in oil, covered, over moderate heat, stirring occasionally, until softened, about 20 minutes. Remove lid and cook onions, stirring occasionally, until golden and any liquid evaporates. Remove skillet from heat to cool onions slightly.

Preheat oven to 375 degrees.

On a lightly floured surface, roll dough 14-inches round. Transfer to a 12-inch tart pan or a 12-inch quiche dish. Spread onion mixture over dough and top with cheese. Arrange tomato wedges and olives in concentric circles over cheese and season with salt and pepper.

Bake tart in middle of oven 1 hour, or until pastry is golden, and cool on a rack. Remove rim of pan. Serve tart warm or at room temperature.

BUTTER PASTRY DOUGH
In a food processor mix the flour and salt together. Add the butter until mixture resembles coarse meal. Add ice water, 1 tablespoon at a time, until mixture begins to form into a dough. Form dough into a disk and chill for 30 minutes.

Serves 10-12

If making this salad for kids you might want to substitute mozzarella or cheddar cheese for the ricotta salata and any greens they like for the mâche.

Mac & Cheese Salad with Buttermilk Dressing

BUTTERMILK DRESSING

1/2 cup mayonnaise
1/2 cup sour cream
1/2 cup buttermilk
1 tablespoon chopped fresh dill
1/4 cup thinly sliced fresh chives
2 teaspoons minced garlic
2 teaspoons minced shallot
2 teaspoons freshly squeezed lemon juice
Salt and freshly ground pepper

SALAD

1 pound fusilli or macaroni
1/4 cup thinly sliced scallion
3 ounces ricotta salata,
grated (about 3/4 cup)
5 cups loosely packed mâche or
baby spinach leaves

Cook the pasta a few hours ahead, run cold water over it, and drain. Drizzle a little olive oil over the pasta and cover with plastic wrap.

To make the buttermilk dressing, whisk together the mayonnaise, sour cream and buttermilk in a bowl. Add the dill, chives, garlic, shallot and lemon juice and whisk again. Season to taste with salt and pepper.

Put the pasta in a large bowl and, using a rubber spatula, fold in enough dressing to coat it generously. Fold in the scallion, cheese and mâche. Mound the salad on a large platter and serve.

NOTE: For variation toss in some blanched and sliced asparagus or blanched fresh peas. The dressing is also good on a salad of poached shrimp, cucumber and Bibb lettuce or mixed into a bowl of steamed and chilled baby red potatoes. Ricotta salata is a slightly tangy Italian sheep's milk cheese. Grate it on the finest holes of a box grater. If not available, substitute pecorino.

Serves 6

Grilled Fig & Arugula Salad with Gorgonzola Toasts

1/3 cup crumbled Gorgonzola cheese
1 tablespoon butter, softened
8 slices crusty bread
12 fresh figs, halved
Cooking spray
2 tablespoons balsamic vinegar
1 tablespoon olive oil
1/2 teaspoon salt
1/4 teaspoon freshly ground black pepper
3 cups baby spinach
3 cups arugula
8 Boston lettuce leaves
2 tablespoons chopped green onions

Preheat the grill.

Combine cheese and butter in small bowl, stir until well blended. Grill bread 5 minutes on each side or until golden; cool. Spread 1 teaspoon cheese mixture on each slice; set aside.

Thread 4 fig halves lengthwise onto each of 6 skewers; coat figs with cooking spray. Place fig kebabs on grill rack, and grill 4 minutes on each side

Cool slightly; remove figs from skewers.

Combine vinegar, oil, salt and pepper in a small bowl. Place spinach arugula and Boston lettuce in a large bowl; add dressing, tossing gently to coat. Divide mixture evenly among 8 serving plates. Top with figs and lettuce leaves; sprinkle wih onions. Serve with grilled bread.

Serves 8

If fresh figs are not available, I buy fig jam and spread it on the toast with the gorgonzola. It's a great substitute.

Grilled Barbecue Shrimp Cobb Salad with Smoked Chile-Buttermilk Dressing

DRESSING

1/4 cup sour cream
1 cup buttermilk
2 cloves garlic, finely chopped
2 tablespoons finely chopped red onion
1 tablespoon fresh lime juice
2 teaspoons chipotle puree
Salt and freshly ground black pepper

SALAD

1 1/2 pounds jumbo shrimp
Salt and pepper
Barbecue sauce
2 large red onions, sliced 1/4-inch thick
Olive oil for brushing the onions
8 cups mixed greens
8 plum tomatoes, quartered
8 hard-boiled eggs, quartered
4 avocados, peeled,
halved and thinly sliced
8 ounces blue cheese, crumbled

Serves 6-8

To ensure sweet, tender shrimp, do not over cook. One, to one and a half minutes is perfect.

DRESSING

Combine the sour cream, buttermilk, garlic, onion, lime juice and chipotle puree in a small bowl and season with salt and pepper. May be refrigerated for 1 day.

SALAD

Preheat a gas or charcoal grill to medium high. Season the shrimp with salt and pepper and brush with barbecue sauce. Grill for about 1 minute on each side. Remove from grill.

Brush the onion slices with olive oil and grill until golden brown and slightly softened, 2 to 3 minutes on each side.

In a large bowl, lightly toss the greens with some of the dressing and place on a large platter. Arrange the shrimp in the center of the platter, resting on the greens. Arrange the tomatoes, eggs, onion slices and avocado slices around the shrimp. Sprinkle with the blue cheese and drizzle with the remainder of the dressing.

NOTE: Chipotles come canned in adobo sauce. If you have a mini prep, puree 1 chipotle for 2 teaspoons. Remove the seeds.

Chop Salad with Corn, Snap Peas & Bacon

FOR THE SALAD

1/2 pound sliced bacon
6 ounces sugar snap peas (1 1/2 cups),
strings removed, cut in half on a diagonal
1 1/2 cups fresh corn kernels
1/2 head romaine
1 medium cucumber, peeled,
seeded and cut into 1/2-inch dice
1/2 medium red bell pepper,
cut into 1/4-inch dice
1 medium carrot, peeled and grated
1/2 bunch radishes, thinly sliced
1/2 bunch scallions, thinly sliced
1/2 pint cherry tomatoes,
stemmed, cut in half
1 cup fresh basil leaves, cut into thin strips
1/2 cup freshly grated Parmesan cheese

MUSTARD VINAIGRETTE

2 tablespoons red wine vinegar
1 tablespoon freshly squeezed lemon juice
1 tablespoon Dijon mustard
2 teaspoons minced garlic
1/2 cup plus 1 tablespoon olive oil
Salt and freshly ground black pepper

A chop salad in the summer time is satisfying and delicious. Crispy and fresh with sweet corn, it can be served alongside a piece of grilled fish or chicken. Perfection!

Fresh Tomato & Goat Cheese Strata with Herb Oil

8 ounces goat cheese
1/4 cup cream
Pinch of salt and freshly ground black pepper
3 fresh tomatoes, sliced 1/2 to 3/4-inch thick
1 cup chopped toasted pine nuts, for garnish

HERB OIL
3/4 cup fresh mint
3/4 cup fresh basil
1 cup olive oil
Pinch of salt and freshly ground black pepper

For the filling combine the goat cheese and cream in a medium bowl. Using an electric mixer, whip together the cheese and the cream. Season with salt and pepper. Set aside.

For the herb oil, combine the herbs in a food processor and pulse to chop the herbs. With the machine running, add the oil, salt and pepper. Transfer to a small bowl. Cover with plastic wrap and set aside.

To serve, using a serrated knife, cut the tomatoes. Top each tomato with a spoonful of the goat cheese mixture. Place a few tomatoes on a serving plate and drizzle with herb oil. Sprinkle with pine nuts and serve.

Serves 6

Whipping the cream and goat cheese together gives a creamy mousse-like consistency. Serve with crusty bread as a great starter to any meal.

Clafouti is a traditional French dessert commonly made with cherries, tomatoes or other fruits and vegetables.

Tomato Clafouti with Green Salad

CLAFOUTI
2 pounds firm, ripe tomatoes
Sea salt to taste
2 large eggs
2 large egg yolks
1/3 cup heavy cream
1/2 cup freshly grated Parmigiano-Reggiano cheese
2 teaspoons fresh thyme leaves

GREEN SALAD
8 cups baby lettuces
2 shallots, thinly sliced
1 cup Nicoise olives
2 tablespoons sherry vinegar
1 1/2 teaspoons Dijon mustard
1/2 cup olive oil

CLAFOUTI

Preheat the oven to 375 degrees.

Core, peel and quarter the tomatoes lengthwise. Place the tomatoes, side by side, on a double thickness of paper towels. Sprinkle generously with fine salt. Cover with another double thickness of paper toweling. Set aside to purge the tomatoes of their liquid for at least 10 minutes and up to 1 hour.

In a small bowl, combine the eggs, egg yolks, cream, half of the cheese and half of the thyme leaves. Season lightly with salt and whisk to blend.

Layer the tomatoes on the bottom of the baking dish. Pour the batter over the tomatoes. Sprinkle with the remaining cheese and thyme. Place in the center of the oven and bake until the batter is set and the clafouti is golden and bubbling, about 30 minutes. Serve warm or at room temperature, cut into wedges.

GREEN SALAD

In a small bowl whisk the sherry and mustard together. Gradually whisk in the olive oil until emulsified. Season with salt and pepper. This makes about 2/3 cup dressing.

Mix all of the salad ingredients together and toss with the vinaigrette. Serve a wedge of the clafouti on top of the salad.

Serves 6

Grilled Antipasto with Gorgonzola Vinaigrette

2 red bell peppers
2 yellow bell peppers
12 ounces medium asparagus, trimmed
2 Japanese eggplants, halved lengthwise
2 small yellow squash, halved lengthwise
2 large portabello mushrooms, stemmed
3/4 cup olive oil
2 teaspoons salt
2 teaspoons freshly ground black pepper
1/2 cup pitted assorted olives
1/4 cup balsamic vinegar
1 teaspoon chopped fresh thyme leaves
4 ounces Gorgonzola cheese, crumbled

Heat your grill to high. Brush the vegetables and mushrooms with 1/4 cup of the oil and season with 1 3/4 teaspoons of the salt and 1 3/4 teaspoons of the pepper. Grill the peppers, turning as needed, until charred on all sides, 8 to 10 minutes. Remove from the grill, place in a bowl covered with plastic wrap and let sit for 15 minutes. Remove and discard the skins, stems and seeds. Then cut the flesh into eighths.

Lay the asparagus crosswise on the grate and turn as needed until just cooked through, 3 minutes per side.

Grill the eggplants and squash cut side down for 3 minutes. Turn them over and continue grilling until just cooked through, 4 to 5 minutes longer. Remove from the grill and cut crosswise into 1/2-inch-thick slices.

Grill the mushrooms for 4 to 5 minutes per side until just cooked through. Remove from the grill and cut into 1/4-inch-thick slices.

Arrange the vegetables on a large platter and scatter the olives around the platter.

Whisk together the vinegar, thyme and remaining 1/4 teapsoon salt and 1/4 teaspoon pepper in a medium bowl. Slowly drizzle in the remaining 1/2 cup olive oil, whisking until emulsified. Stir in the Gorgonzola.

Drizzle the vinaigrette over the vegetables; serve warm or at room temperature.

Serves 6

Summer Peach, Mozzarella & Basil Stacks

3 large ripe peaches
1 pound fresh mozzarella
Basil leaves
Salt and freshly ground black pepper
3 tablespoons olive oil
Reduced balsamic vinegar for drizzling

Cut the peaches in half, remove the seed and slice into rounds.

Slice the mozzarella into rounds and choose basil leaves to layer in between the peaches and cheese.

Place one layer of peach, mozzarella, basil leaf and repeat two more times stacking the slices. Drizzle the olive oil and balsamic vinegar on and around the stacks. Serve immediately.

NOTE: To reduce balsamic vinegar, place in a saucepan over medium heat. Reduce until it is a syrup consistency.

Serves 6

This classic is usually made with tomatoes but works beautifully with peaches or plums. The colors are great.

Margarita Shrimp Salad with Creamy Lime-Chile Dressing

1 1/2 pounds cooked shrimp
1/4 cup tequila
2 teaspoons freshly grated orange zest
1 teaspoon freshly grated lime zest
1/2 teaspoon salt
1/4 cup thinly sliced red onion
1/2 cup Creamy Lime-Chile Dressing
6 cups washed, dried and torn baby Romaine lettuce
2 medium endives, torn into pieces
1 orange, peeled and cut into segments
2 ripe Hass avacados, peeled, pitted and cut into cubes
1 tablespoon fresh lime juice
1 tablespoon olive oil
Lime wedges

CREAMY LIME-CHILE DRESSING
(Makes about 1/2 cup)
6 tablespoons sour cream
3 tablespoons fresh lime juice
2 teaspoons minced seeded jalapeño
1 teaspoon chili powder
1 teaspoon sugar
1/4 teaspoon salt

Toss shrimp, tequila, orange zest, lime zest and salt in a medium bowl. Cover and marinate in the refrigerator for 10 minutes, stirring occasionally. Place onion in a small bowl, cover with cold water and some ice; let stand for 10 minutes, or until ready to use.

Meanwhile, make the dressing by whisking all of the ingredients in a small bowl.

Toss romaine, endive, orange segments and onion in a large bowl. Add dressing and toss to coat. Toss the avocado with lime juce and add to the bowl. Add the shrimp and marinade to the bowl. Serve with lime wedges.

Serves 6

A great tip for cooking shrimp: Clean and devein, bring a pot of water to a boil, turn the heat off and add raw shrimp for exactly 5 minutes. Remove and run cold water until cool. Do not cover.

Fresh Fig, Prosciutto & Arugula Salad with Parmesan Shavings

2 tablespoons balsamic vinegar
1/2 teaspoon Dijon mustard
Freshly ground pepper to taste
6 tablespoons olive oil

2 large bunches arugula
6 firm-ripe green or purple figs
6-8 large thin prosciutto slices
Parmigiano-Reggiano cheese

The figs and prosciutto also work well grilled. The charred flavor is spectacular, salty and sweet. Try substituting gorgonzola for the parmesan.

In a bowl whisk together vinegar, mustard, pepper and salt to taste. In a slow stream whisk in oil until emulsified.

Discard stems from arugula and transfer to a large bowl. Trim tough ends from figs and cut each fig into 8 wedges. Halve 6 prosciutto slices lengthwise. Overlap narrow ends of 2 halves by 1 to 2 inches, pressing together gently to form 6 pieces about 13 inches long. Transfer long prosciutto pieces as prepared to a tray lined with plastic wrap. With a vegetable peeler shave about 36 thin slices from Parmigiano-Reggiano.

Toss arugula with about 3 tablespoons vinaigrette and mound in center of each of 6 plates. Arrange long prosciutto pieces in a ring around each mound of arugula, overlapping ends to secure. Arrange figs and cheese shavings on and around salad and drizzle salads with remaining vinaigrette.

Serves 6

Orzo Salad with Shrimp, Roasted Peppers, Corn & Grilled Portabellos

1 pound orzo
1 pound large shrimp, peeled and deveined
1 large poblano chili pepper
1 small red bell pepper
2 large plum tomatoes, seeded and chopped
1 cup fresh corn kernels
1/3 cup chopped fresh cilantro
1/4 cup chopped green onions
2 1/2 tablespoons fresh lime juice
2 tablespoons olive oil
6 portabello mushrooms
6 cups baby spinach

Cook the orzo. Drain. (May be prepared a day ahead and placed in a zip-lock bag tossed with a little olive oil until ready to use.)

Char the poblano and red bell pepper under the broiler until blackened on all sides. Enclose in a plastic bag and let stand 10 minutes. Peel, seed and dice poblano and red pepper.

Place the orzo, poblano and red pepper in a large bowl. Add the tomatoes, corn, cilantro, onions, lime juice, and olive oil and toss to blend. Season salad with salt and pepper

Prepare the barbecue. Spray mushrooms and shrimp with canola oil and sprinkle with salt and pepper. Grill until cooked through, about 4 minutes per side. Transfer to a work surface; slice the mushrooms. The shrimp will take about 2 minutes total.

Arrange baby spinach leaves on each of the plates. Top with orzo salad. Arrange mushrooms and shrimp on each salad.

Alternatively, mix the spinach leaves with the orzo salad and serve on whole grilled mushrooms.

Serves 6

Subsitute any pasta that you have on hand. Macaroni or penne also work well.

Any mix of seafood is good. Leave out the calamari, if you want, and add sea scallops. Grilled salmon is also very good.

Neapolitan Vegetable Seafood Salad

4 cups chicken broth
1/2 pound orzo pasta
1/2 pound calamari
1/2 pound shrimp or
1 pound mixed seafood (1 bag frozen)
2 zucchini, sliced lengthwise,
about 1-inch wide
1 Japanese eggplant, sliced lengthwise,
about 1-inch wide.
2 Roma tomatoes, halved lengthwise
1 (15-ounce) can cannellini beans,
drained and rinsed
3 ounces arugula (about 3 cups)
3/4 cups chopped fresh basil leaves
1/4 cup chopped fresh flat-leaf parsley
2 lemons, juiced
2/3 cup olive oil
1 1/2 teaspoons salt
1 1/2 teaspoons freshly ground
black pepper

In a large pot, bring the chicken broth to a boil over high heat. Add the pasta and cook until tender but still firm to the bite, stirring occasionally, about 8 to 10 minutes. Drain the pasta and place in a large bowl.

Meanwhile, place a grill pan over medium-high heat or preheat a gas or charcoal grill.

Drizzle the fish, zucchini, eggplant and tomatoes with olive oil and season with salt and pepper. Grill the seafood, just until cooked through, about 1 to 2 minutes per side. Grill the zucchini and eggplant until tender, about 4 minutes per side. Grill the tomatoes just until grill marks appear, about 2 minutes.

Add the orzo, cannellini beans, arugula, basil and parsley to the bowl. Cut the zucchini, eggplant and tomatoes into roughly about 1-inch cubes. Add the vegetables and seafood to the bowl with the lemon juice, olive oil, salt and pepper. Toss to combine. Serve this salad on a large platter with grilled crusty bread.

Serves 6

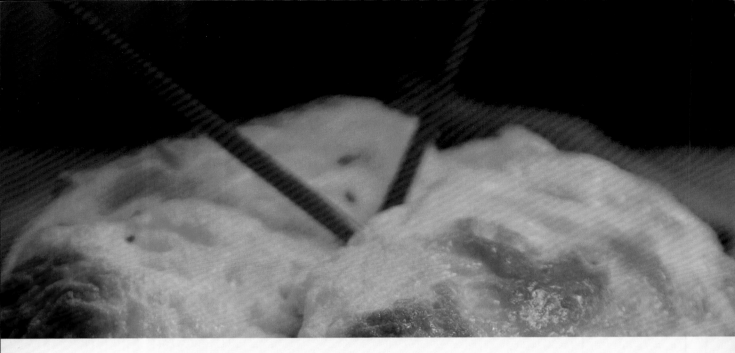

SERRANO SOUFFLÉS

1 tablespoon butter
2 tablespoons panko
2 tablespoons finely chopped
toasted pine nuts
2 tablespoons butter
1 tablespoon finely chopped shallots
2 serrano chiles,
seeded and finely chopped
2 tablespoons flour
1/2 cup milk
2 egg yolks
1 cup grated Gruyère cheese
Salt and pepper to taste
6 egg whites

DRESSING

2 tablespoons balsamic vinegar
1/2 cup walnut oil
Salt and pepper to taste
9 cups spring lettuce mix
2 red pears, julienned
1/2 cup toasted pine nuts

Serrano Soufflés on Greens with Pears & Pine Nuts

To prepare the soufflés, preheat oven to 400 degrees. Butter 8 individual 1/2 cup ramekins. Mix bread crumbs and finely chopped piñon nuts together and coat inside of buttered ramekins with the mixture; put in a baking dish and chill until ready to fill.

Melt 2 tablespoons butter in a saucepan. Add shallots, chiles and flour and cook, stirring constantly, for 3 minutes. Add milk and cook, whisking constantly, until thick. Remove from heat and add egg yolks, mix thoroughly. Stir in cheese and season with salt and pepper.

In a separate bowl, whip egg whites until soft peaks form. Fold into the cheese mixture and divide among the chilled ramekins. Fill the baking dish with enough hot water to go half way up the sides of the ramekins. Bake until the soufflés are puffed and golden, about 15 to 20 minutes.

Place the vinegar in a bowl and season with salt and pepper. slowly whisk in the oil. Set aside.

Toss the greens with the vinaigrette. Unmold the soufflés and place in the middle of the greens. Slice the pears and place around the soufflé. Sprinkle toasted pine nuts on top.

Serves 8

Butternut Squash Salad with Pine Nuts, Shaved Pecorino & Balsamic Vinegar

2 pounds butternut squash
2 tablespoons fresh marjoram
2 cloves garlic
1 1/2 teaspoons salt
1 teaspoon ground cumin
1/4 teaspoon cinnamon
1/4 teaspoon coriander
1/4 cup olive oil
3 tablespoons fresh lemon juice
3 tablespoons of pine nuts, lightly toasted
Sea salt
1/8 teaspoon cayenne pepper
8 cups arugula
1 wedge Pecorino Romano cheese
(about 4 ounces)
Aged balsamic vinegar and olive oil for
drizzling

This is a beautiful salad. The perfect combination of spice and vinegar

Preheat oven to 400 degrees. Peel, seed, and cut squash into 1 1/2-inch chunks. Using a mini food processor chop the marjoram, garlic, and cumin. Add 2 tablespoons olive oil and mix to form a paste.

In a large bowl, toss squash in spice paste. On a parchment-lined, rimmed baking sheet, spread pumpkin in a single layer and bake for about 40 minutes. Cool slightly.

Return squash to bowl and drizzle with 1 tablespoon olive oil and 2 tablespoons lemon juice. Add pine nuts, salt, and ground red pepper. Toss gently to combine.

Arrange 1/3 of the squash on a serving platter. In the bowl with the remaining squash, add arugula, the rest of the olive oil and lemon juice, and salt to taste; toss gently. Top plated squash with arugula mixture. Cut cheese into thin wedges or shave with a vegetable peeler and arrange on top of salad. Drizzle with balsamic vinegar and olive oil to taste.

Serves 6

If tangerine juice is not available use orange juice.

2 cups freshly squeezed tangerine juice
2 tangerines
1 tablespoon coarsely
chopped fresh tarragon
1 egg yolk
Salt and freshly ground pepper
1 cup olive oil, plus more for tossing with
and brushing on
asparagus and greens

2 large bunches of asparagus, about 2
pounds, trimmed and
blanched for about 3 minutes
Long curls of tangerine zest
Toasted pine nuts for garnish
6 cups baby lettuces

Grilled Asparagus with Tangerine Mayonnaise, Toasted Pine Nuts & Baby Lettuces

Put the juice in a small nonreactive saucepan and bring to a boil. Cook until reduced to 1/2 cup. Let cool. Peel the tangerines, removing all the white pith, and segment over a bowl to catch both the segments and the juices. Cover and refrigerate until very cold.

Combine the reduced juice, tarragon, egg yolk and salt and pepper to taste in a blender and blend until well mixed. With the machine running, add the 1 cup olive oil, at first by drops and then, as mixture emulsifies, in a thin, steady stream until all the oil is incorporated. Taste for seasoning. Scrape into a jar, cover, and refrigerate until needed. You should have about 1 2/3 cups. (Keeps 2 to 3 days, refrigerated.)

Prepare the grill. Toss the asparagus with 1 tablespoon olive oil and season with salt and pepper. Grill over medium heat, turning the spears as needed.

Arrange the asparagus on a platter with the reserved tangerine segments. Dot with the mayonnaise, and drizzle with any tangerine juice left in the bowl.

Garnish with the zest and pine nuts.

Arrange the greens that have been tossed with olive oil around the outside of the platter.

NOTE: The mayonnaise tastes great on all kinds of vegetables and on poached fish. It can also be used to bind a chicken salad or as a sandwich spread.

Serves 6

Three-Pea Salad with Manchego & Ham

1 tablespoon minced shallot
1 tablespoon sherry vinegar
1 tablespoon crème fraîche or sour cream
1/4 cup olive oil
Salt and freshly ground pepper
1/2 pound sugar snap peas
1/2 cup snow peas, halved crosswise
One 10-ounce box frozen baby peas
Manchego cheese, cut into cubes
3-ounce package
Serrano ham cut into cubes

Bring a large saucepan of salted water to a boil. Fill a large bowl with ice water. In another large bowl, whisk the shallot, vinegar and sour cream together. Whisk in the olive oil until emulsified. Season with salt and pepper.

Add the sugar snap peas to the boiling water and blanch for 20 seconds. Add the snow peas and cook for 20 seconds. Add the frozen baby peas and cook for 20 seconds longer, until the sugar snaps and snow peas are crisp, tender and the baby peas are heated through.

Drain and immediately transfer the colander to the ice water to stop the cooking. Drain again and pat the peas dry. Add the peas to the dressing. Fold in the ham and cubes of Manchego and gently toss together. Season with salt and pepper and toss again.

I'm not sure why, but I love cornbread with this salad. If you make it in a cast iron skillet, it gets very crispy on the bottom.

Hearts of Romaine with Maytag Blue Cheese, Toasted Chile Pecans & Sliced Pear

4 heads romaine lettuce
MAYTAG BLUE DRESSING
1/2 cup Maytag blue cheese crumbled
1/2 cup sour cream
1/2 cup buttermilk
1/4 cup half-and-half
2 ounces soft goat cheese (1/4 cup)
Juice from 1 orange
1 tablespoon minced,
stemmed fresh mint leaves
2 tablespoons minced,
stemmed fresh basil leaves
1 small shallot, minced
1/4 teaspoon salt
1/4 teaspoon cayenne pepper
Freshly ground black pepper
CHILE PECANS
1 cup pecan halves
2 tablespoons canola oil
2 teaspoons Kahlua liqueur
1 heaping tablespoon
good quality chile powder
2 teaspoons granulated sugar
2 ripe but firm pears,
cored and sliced lengthwise
Coarse-ground black pepper
3 lemons, halved and seeded

Use only the hearts of the romaine lettuces. Separate, wash and dry the leaves. May serve whole or torn into bite size pieces.

To prepare the dressing: In a salad bowl combine all the ingredients, including black pepper, and mix throughly. Taste and adjust seasonings. Cover and refrigerate.

For the pecans: Preheat the oven to 300 degrees. In a bowl toss the nuts with the oil and Kahlua liqueur until evenly coated. Add the chile powder and sugar and toss again. Spread the nuts out on a baking sheet and place in the oven, stirring frequently, until toasted, about 25 minutes. Do not allow them to burn. Set aside to cool.

To assemble the salad: Toss the romaine leaves with the dressing until every leaf is coated. Place on individual plates and sprinkle the pecans over the leaves. Fan the pear slices on top of the romaine leaves. Grind black pepper over all, then squeeze half a lemon over each salad.

Serve immediately.

Serves 6

Serve these tomatoes for brunch. Add scrambled eggs to the plate and you have a beautiful dish for brunch.

6 ripe medium tomatoes
Salt
4 teaspoons butter
1 1/2 tablespoons minced shallots
2 teaspoons minced garlic
1 1/2 tablespoons flour
1/3 cup half-and-half
1 tablespoon dry sherry
1/2 cup fresh, soft goat cheese

2 eggs, separated
3 tablespoons minced fresh chives
2 teaspoons minced tarragon
Freshly ground white pepper
4 cups mixed savory baby greens

LEMON-GARLIC
VINAIGRETTE
3 tablespoons white wine vinegar
1 tablespoon fresh lemon juice
2 teaspoons Dijon mustard
1/2 teaspoon roasted garlic
1/2 teaspoon salt
1 tablespoon light-brown sugar or honey
1/2 cup olive oil

Souffléed Goat Cheese Tomatoes & Savory Greens with Lemon-Garlic Vinaigrette

Slice the tops off the tomatoes and scoop out the seeds and pulp. Sprinkle the insides with salt and invert the tomatoes on paper towels to drain.

In a small saucepan, melt the butter. Add the shallots and garlic and saute until soft but not brown. Add the flour and continue cooking for 2-3 minutes, stirring continuously. Whisk in the half-and-half and the sherry, cooking for 3 minutes longer and continuously whisking until the mixture is smooth. Transfer the mixture to a bowl and let cool slightly. Whisk in the goat cheese, egg yolks, chives, tarragon, salt and pepper.

In a separate bowl, beat the egg whites until they hold stiff peaks. Stir 1/4 of the whites into the cheese mixture to lighten it. Carefully fold in the remaining whites.

Preheat the oven to 400 degrees. Spoon the soufflé mixture into the tomato shells, mounding it slightly. Place the tomatoes, with their sides touching, in a lightly oiled baking dish. Bake for 20-25 minutes or until the tops are lightly puffed and browned.

Serve the hot tomatoes immediately on a bed of the mixed greens on chilled plates. Drizzle with about 1/4 cup of the vinaigrette and finish with a sprinkling of white pepper.

LEMON-GARLIC VINAIGRETTE

In a bowl, whisk together all the ingredients. Store any unused vinaigrette tightly covered in the refrigerator for up to 5 days.

Serves 6

The contrasting color of salmon with
the asparagus is so appealing.

Try presenting this salad on a dinner
plate.

Grilled Asparagus with Smoked Salmon & Tarragon Mayonnaise on Bitter Greens

1 1/2 pounds asparagus
1/2 pound smoked salmon, thinly sliced
1 lemon, cut into wedges
6 cups bitter greens

TARRAGON MAYONNAISE
3/4 cup mayonnaise
1/4 cup minced fresh tarragon
1 teaspoon lemon juice
1 teaspoon olive oil
1/4 teaspoon salt

NOTE: In place of the smoked salmon, use an equal amount of thinly sliced prosciutto.

Prepare a grill by preheating.

Break off any tough ends from the asparagus, then trim ends with a knife. Blanch the asparagus in boiling water for about 2 minutes. Drain, rinse with cold running water until cool, and drain again.

When the grill is hot, place the asparagus on the grill, turning as needed, until lightly marked and just tender, 2-3 minutes on each side.

To make the tarragon mayonnaise, place the mayonnaise in a bowl. Add the tarragon, lemon juice, oil and salt and stir to mix well. Cover and refrigerate until serving.

To serve, lightly dress the bitter greens with olive oil, lemon juice and salt and pepper. Place some of the greens at the top of the plate. Make a bed of the salmon slices on each plate, dividing the salmon evenly. Arrange the grilled asparagus on top of the salmon along with some tarragon mayonnaise, again dividing evenly. Garnish with lemon wedges.

Serves 6

Caesar Salad with Red Chile Croutons

This has to be one of my favorite Caesar salads. The chipotles in the dressing add a smoky flavor that really works.

4 cups green romaine lettuce,
inner leaves only
1/2 cup Spicy Caesar Dressing
Red Chile Croutons
1/4 cup grated Parmesan
12 leaves red romaine lettuce
or baby romaine

RED CHILE CROUTONS
8 slices French or Italian bread,
1/2-inch thick
1/4 cup olive oil
1 teaspoon ancho chile powder
Salt and freshly ground pepper to taste

SPICY CAESAR DRESSING
1 egg yolk
1 teaspoon Dijon mustard
1 teaspoon freshly ground pepper
1 teaspoon pureed canned chipotles
1 teaspoon Worchestershire sauce
Few drops Tabasco sauce
1 tablespoon fresh lime juice
1 teaspoon capers
10 anchovy filets
8 garlic cloves, roasted or lightly sauteed
1 1/2 cups olive oil
1 tablespoon red wine vinegar

Place the green romaine in a large bowl, add the dressing, croutons, and half the Parmesan and toss together.

Divide the salad among 4 individual bowls, sprinkle with the remaining Parmesan and arrange the red romaine leaves, if available, in the center of each serving.

RED CHILE CROUTONS
Preheat the oven to 350 degrees. Toss the bread with the olive oil and place on a baking sheet. Sprinkle with the chile powder and salt and pepper to taste. Bake for about 7 minutes, or until lightly browned.

SPICY CAESAR DRESSING
Put all the ingredients, except the oil and vinegar, in a food processor and process until coarsely blended. Transfer to a mixing bowl.

Slowly mix in the oil, then mix in the vinegar. If the dressing is very thick, mix in a little water. May be prepared up to 1 day ahead and refrigerated in a squeeze bottle. Bring to room temperature before serving.

Serves 6

Salad Greens & Deep Fried Vegetable Ribbons

DEEP FRIED VEGETABLES
4 cups vegetable oil
Skins from a 2-pound eggplant,
cut 1/8-inch thick and julienned;
reserve eggplant flesh for another purpose
Salt and freshly ground black pepper
3/4 cup leeks, white part only, julienned

SALAD & VINAIGRETTE
Mixed young salad greens
12 fresh tarragon leaves, roughly chopped
12 fresh mint leaves, roughly chopped
8 fresh basil leaves, roughly chopped
1 tablespoon finely chopped dill
2 teaspoons finely chopped fresh cilantro
1 shallot, finely chopped
4 tablespoons balsamic vinegar
3 tablespoons water
Salt and freshly ground pepper
1/2 cup olive oil

Heat the vegetable oil in a large, deep skillet to 375 degrees. Fry the eggplant until crisp, about 8 to 10 minutes. Drain on paper towels. Season with salt and pepper to taste. Repeat the process with the leeks. Set aside.

Place mixed salad greens, tarragon, mint leaves, basil, dill, cilantro and shallots in a bowl. Set aside.

Mix the vinegar, water, salt and pepper to taste in a small bowl. Gradually whisk in olive oil. Set aside.

To serve, toss the salad greens with the vinaigrette in a bowl. Evenly divide among 6 plates and top with the deep fried vegetables.

I really like this salad with a grilled steak. All of the flavors work well together.

Italian Salad with Bocconcini & Green Olive Tapenade

3 tablespoons green olive
tapenade from a jar
1/4 cup peperoncini stemmed,
seeded and finely chopped
1/2 cup olive oil
1 1/2 cups bocconcini
(small balls of mozzarella)
1 tablespoon plus 1 teaspoon
fresh lemon juice
1 tablespoon plus 1 teaspoon
red wine vinegar
1 tablespoon plus 1 teaspoon
minced garlic
1 teaspoon dried oregano
Salt and freshly ground pepper
1 small head of iceberg lettuce, halved,
cored and finely shredded
6 ounces thinly sliced Genoa salami,
cut into thin strips
6 small basil leaves
1/2 cup green olives, such as Picholine

In a medium bowl, mix the green olive tapenade with the peperoncini and 1/4 cup of the oil. Add the bocconcini and toss.

In a small bowl, whisk the lemon juice with the vinegar, garlic and oregano. Whisk in the remaining 1/4 cup of olive oil and season the dressing with salt and pepper.

In a large bowl, combine the shredded lettuce and salami. Add the marinated bocconcini and half of the dressing and toss well. Transfer the antipasto salad to a large platter. Top with the basil and olives. Drizzle the remaining dressing around the salad and serve at once.

Serves 8

*Have a pizza delivered and serve it with this salad.
Great for Monday Night Football.*

Peppery Greens with Mango, Tortillas & Orange Vinaigrette

6 cups bitter or peppery greens
1 large ripe mango, peeled,
seeded and diced
Three 6-inch tortillas
1 cup vegetable oil
1/2 cup Orange Vinaigrette

ORANGE VINAIGRETTE
1 cup fresh orange juice
2 tablespoons chopped red onion
2 tablespoons fresh lime juice
1 teaspoon Dijon mustard
1 teaspoon ancho chile powder
1 tablespoon red wine vinegar
1/2 cup olive oil
Salt and freshly ground pepper

The secret to this great salad is reducing the orange juice to a syrup. It becomes very concentrated and flavorful.

To make the vinaigrette: In a saucepan over high heat, reduce the orange juice until it forms a syrup. Let the syrup cool slightly.

In a blender, combine the orange syrup, onion, lime juice, mustard, chile powder and vinegar. Blend for 30 seconds. With the blender running, slowly add the olive oil until the dressing emulsifies. Season with salt and pepper. Pour into a squeeze bottle. May be prepared 1 day ahead and refrigerated. Bring to room temperature before serving.

For the tortilla strips: In a saucepan over high heat, heat the oil to about 375 degrees, or until a tortilla strip sizzles when it is immersed. Fry the tortilla strips for 10 to 20 seconds, or until crisp, and drain on paper towels.

In a mixing bowl, dress the greens very lightly with the orange vinaigrette. Combine the greens, mango and tortilla strips, being careful not to break the strips.

NOTE: This salad is good served with seared scallops on top, or shrimp.

Serves 6

Arugula Salad with Crisp Fingerling Potato Chips

6 slices of bacon cut into 1-inch pieces
2 tablespoons balsamic vinegar
2 teaspoons Dijon mustard
1 shallot, finely chopped
Salt and freshly ground black pepper
1/2 cup olive oil
6 ounces crumbled blue cheese
8 cups arugula
1 pound fingerling potatoes
Canola oil for chips

Cook the bacon in a skillet until crispy. Drain the bacon on paper towels.

In a small bowl, combine the vinegar, mustard and shallot, and season with salt and pepper to taste. Whisk in the olive oil in a steady stream until it is incorporated and an emulsion forms.

Slice the fingerling potatoes paper thin with a mandolin. Dry between paper towels. Heat the canola oil to about 375 degrees. Fry the potato chips in the hot oil until golden brown. Remove and drain on paper towels. Season with sea salt.

Toss the arugula with just enough dressing to coat lightly. Add the bacon pieces and blue cheese. Serve the salad with the potato chips on the top.

NOTE: Potato chips may be prepared ahead of time and stored in an airtight container.

Serves 6

This salad is great to serve on hamburger night. That includes turkey or salmon burgers as well.

Cheddar, Pear & Walnut Salad
with Pear Vinaigrette

3/4 cup coarsely chopped toasted walnuts
2 firm Bartlett pears, peeled, cored and sliced
8 cups Boston or Bibb lettuce, torn into large pieces
6 ounces (1 1/2 cups) crumbled white extra sharp cheddar cheese

PEAR VINAIGRETTE
1 firm Bartlett pear, peeled, cored and quartered
1 tablespoon walnut oil
3 tablespoons olive oil
4 teaspoons sherry vinegar
1/2 teaspoon balsamic vinegar
1/8 teaspoon salt

To make the vinaigrette, puree pear, oils, vinegars and salt together in a blender or food processor.

Toss the walnuts, pears and lettuce in a large bowl with dressing. Divide among plates and garnish with the crumbled cheese.

Serves 6

Adding the pear to the vinaigrette makes it very creamy and smooth.

Red Lettuces with Spiced Almonds, Picholines & Asiago

1 shallot, minced
3 tablespoons fresh lemon juice
1/4 cup chopped chives
1/2 teaspoon freshly ground pepper
Salt
1/3 cup walnut oil
12 cups cleaned red lettuces
(red romaine, red oak leaf & radicchio)
1/2 cup grated Parmesan
32 picholine olives
1/2 cup spiced almonds
8 thin slices asiago cheese

In a small mixing bowl, whisk together the shallot, lemon juice, chives, pepper and salt to taste. Slowly whisk in the walnut oil. Set aside.

Put the lettuces, Parmesan, olives and almonds in a large salad bowl. Toss to combine. Add the dressing and toss to dress thoroughly. Adjust seasoning.

Divide the lettuce among the salad plates. Be sure the olives and almonds are evenly divided. Lean 2 slices of the asiago against each of the salads.

(See next page for the spiced almonds.)

Serves 6

If you don't have time to make the spiced almonds, use Spanish Marcona olives instead.

Spiced Almonds

Vegetable oil spray
1 pound blanched almonds
1/4 cup sugar
1 tablespoon ground cinnamon
1/4 teaspoon sweet paprika
Cayenne
2 tablespoons honey

Preheat the oven to 350 degrees. Spray a shallow baking sheet with vegetable spray. Spread the almonds in a single layer and toast for 15 minutes, or until browned but not too dark. Remove and let cool. Keep the oven turned on.

Meanwhile, in a small bowl, mix together the sugar, cinnamon and paprika. Season to taste with cayenne. When the nuts are cool, drizzle with honey and toss.

Sprinkle the spice mixture on the nuts. Put back in the oven for 5-10 minutes. Remove and let cool. Store in an airtight container at room temperature for a week.

Noodle Salad with
Spicy Peanut Butter Dressing

6 tablespoons creamy peanut butter
1/4 cup chicken broth
3 tablespoons rice vinegar
3 tablespoons soy sauce
1 1/2 tablespoons sugar
1 tablespoon sesame oil
1 tablespoon minced,
 peeled fresh ginger
1/2 teaspoon cayenne pepper
8 ounces linguine
1 large orange bell pepper, cut into
 matchstick-size strips
1/2 cup chopped green onions
5 large lettuce leaves (Butter lettuce)
1/4 cup chopped fresh cilantro
1/4 cup chopped salted peanuts

Combine dressing ingredients in a small bowl; whisk to blend. Set dressing aside.

Cook the pasta in a large pot of boiling salted water until just tender but still firm to the bite, stirring occasionally, about 8 minutes. Drain pasta; rinse with cold water and drain again. Transfer pasta to a medium bowl. Add the bell pepper and green onions. Pour the dressing over and toss to coat. Season with salt and pepper.

Line a serving bowl with lettuce leaves. Transfer salad to prepared bowl. Sprinkle with cilantro and peanuts.

Serves 6

Serve this salad with grilled shrimp or chicken for a complete meal.
It's flavorful, colorful and delicious.

Chipotle-Chicken Salad with Charred Corn & Black Beans

VINAIGRETTE
1/3 cup chopped fresh cilantro
2/3 cup sour cream
1 tablespoon minced chipotle chile,
  canned in adobo sauce
1 teaspoon ground cumin
1 teaspoon chili powder
4 teaspoons fresh lime juice
1/4 teaspoon salt

SALAD
4 cups shredded romaine lettuce
1 roasted chicken, remove skin and bones
1 cup cherry tomatoes, halved
1 diced avocado
1/2 red onion, sliced thinly
1 (15-ounce) can black beans,
  rinsed and drained
4 ears corn, charred under the broiler

6 corn tortillas, sliced and
cooked until crispy in canola oil

Mix all of the ingredients for the vinaigrette in the bowl of a blender.

Combine all of the ingredients for the salad in a large bowl. Drizzle with the dressing and toss gently to coat. Serve immediately topped with taco strips.

Serves 6

It is so easy to purchase roasted chickens these days. I add them to salads, pot pies, enchiladas and lasagne. They are inexpensive and delicious.

Winter

Caramelized Onion & Jalapeño Waffles with Smoked Salmon, Radish Salad & Lemon Cream

CARAMELIZED ONIONS
3 tablespoons unsalted butter
2 yellow onions, finely diced
1 jalapeño chile, seeded and minced

LEMON CREAM
1 cup crème fraîche
1/4 cup milk
Grated zest of 1 lemon
5 tablespoons fresh lemon juice
1/2 teaspoon salt
1 teaspoon sugar

RADISH SALAD
8 ounces mixed salad greens
2 bunches radishes,
trimmed and thinly sliced
3 green onions, including light green parts,
finely chopped
5 tablespoons fresh lemon juice
2 tablespoons olive oil
1 1/2 teaspoons Dijon mustard
Salt and freshly ground pepper

WAFFLES
2 cups all purpose flour
1/2 cup mixed minced fresh herbs, such as
parsley, thyme, chives
1 1/2 tablespoon baking powder
1/2 teaspoon freshly ground pepper
1 teaspoon salt
1 1/2 cups milk
2 eggs at room temperature, beaten
1/3 cup clarified butter, melted
4 ounces thinly sliced smoked salmon

The waffles make a great appetizer with the smoked salmon and lemon cream.

In a large saute pan, melt the butter over medium heat. Add the onions and jalapeño and saute until the onions are caramelized, about 10 minutes. Set aside.

In a medium bowl, combine all the ingredients for the lemon cream and whisk to blend. Cover and refrigerate.

In a medium bowl, combine the salad greens, radishes, and green onions. In a small mixing bowl, combine the lemon juice, olive oil, mustard, and salt and pepper to taste. Whisk to blend.

To make waffles: In a large bowl, combine the flour, herbs, baking powder, pepper, and salt. Stir to blend. In a separate bowl, combine the milk, eggs, and clarified butter and whisk thoroughly. Fold the wet ingredients into the dry ingredients just until moistened. The batter should be slightly lumpy. Fold in the caramelized onion mixture. Chill.

Heat the waffle iron according to the manufacturer's instructions. Spray with cooking spray. Cook the waffle batter, being careful not to overfill the iron, until golden brown, 6 to 7 minutes. Transfer to a plate and keep warm in a low oven while cooking the remaining batter.

To serve, place 2 waffle squares slightly overlapping in the center of each plate. Roll the smoked salmon into tubes and place them beside the waffles. Toss the salad with the dressing and top each waffle with a salad portion. Drizzle the entire plate with lemon cream.

NOTE: You may substitute caviar for the salmon. If using caviar, dollop a tiny amount into the lemon cream. Frozen waffles work well. Add the herbs to the lemon cream.

The salty pancetta is delicious with the asparagus. This
salad is great for lunch if you add a can of albacore tuna.

Arugula with Pancetta,
Grilled Asparagus & White Beans

1/2 cup olive oil
1/2 cup red wine vinegar
1/3 cup freshly grated Parmesan
2 cloves garlic
1 tablespoon freshly ground
black pepper
2 tablespoons roughly chopped fresh basil
16 spears asparagus,
bottom 2 inches trimmed
1 tablespoon olive oil
Salt and pepper to taste
2 bunces arugula, trimmed,
washed and dried
1 cup cooked (or canned) white beans
(rinsed if canned)
1 small red onion,
peeled and diced small
1/2 pound pancetta, thinly sliced, cooked
in a 350 degree oven for 6 to 8 minutes,
or until crispy (or subsitute bacon), and
drained on paper towels.

Make the dressing: In a food processor or blender, combine all of the ingredients except the basil and puree until smooth. Transfer to a bowl, stir in the basil, cover, and refrigerate. (This dressing will keep, covered and refrigerated, for about a week.)

Fill the sink or large pot with ice and water. In a large pot of boiling water, blanch the asparagus until just tender, about 3 minutes. Drain, plunge into the ice water to stop cooking and drain again.

Rub the asparagus lightly with the oil, sprinkle with salt and pepper to taste, and grill over a medium-hot fire, turning frequently for 3 to 5 minutes or until seared.

In a medium bowl, combine the arugula, white beans and onion. Stir the dressing, then pour just enough on the arugula-bean mixture to moisten. Toss well, place on a serving platter, top with the pancetta and asparagus, and serve.

Serves 6

Bibb Salad with Lemon Vinaigrette & Shower of Bleu Cheese

2 heads Boston Bibb lettuce
1/2 cup pine nuts,toasted
and placed in 1/4 cup olive oil
8-10 ounces bleu cheese, cut into small
blocks and frozen
1/4 cup lemon juice
1/4 cup olive oil
1/2 red onion, shaved thin
1 bunch mâche
Salt and pepper

Gently clean lettuce. Remove the core. Wash and gently let dry. Toast the pine nuts and combine with 1/4 cup olive oil.

Mix together the olive oil and lemon juice. Season with salt and pepper. Gently toss lettuce in a bowl with the vinaigrette.

Stack on a plate. Top with a spoonful of the pine nut and oil mixture. Add a pinch of red onion.

Generously grate the bleu cheese over the salad with micro plane grater. Garnish with a little of the mâche and serve.

Serves 6

This salad is the perfect palate cleanser before starting the main course or serving after. Either way it is light and delicious.

Mixed Greens with Shaved Manchego Cheese & Sherry Vinaigrette

2 teaspoons Dijon mustard
2 tablespoons Spanish sherry vinegar
1/4 cup olive oil
Salt and freshly ground black pepper
6 cups mixed greens
2 ounces manchego cheese

Combine the mustard and vinegar in a mixing bowl and whisk to blend. Slowly add the olive oil in a thin stream, whisking constantly, until mixture thickens. Season with salt and pepper to taste.

Put the mixed greens in a large bowl and drizzle with vinaigrette. Put the dressed greens on serving plates and top with a few grinds of black pepper and a sprinkle of salt. Use a cheese shaver or vegetable peeler to shave cheese into thin shards. Distribute cheese over each salad and serve.

Serves 6

Manchego is a Spanish cheese. It has a salty, nutty flavor that is great in a salad or served with almonds as an hors d'oeuvre.

Nicoise Salad with Tarragon Vinaigrette

3/4 cup olive oil
1/4 cup sherry wine vinegar
1 cup thinly sliced fennel bulb
(save 1 tablespoon
snipped fronds for the dressing)
1 tablespoon chopped tarragon
1 teaspoon Dijon mustard
1 teaspoon salt
1/4 teaspoon freshly ground black pepper
1 (5-ounce) bag baby spinach or mâche
1 (12-ounce) can solid white
albacore tuna, drained
1 1/2 cups grape or
cherry tomatoes, halved
1 (6-ounce) jar marinated
artichoke hearts, drained
1/4 cup whole pitted nicoise olives
4 hard-cooked eggs

For the vinaigrette, combine the oil, vinegar, reserved 1 tablespoon fennel fronds, tarragon, mustard, salt and pepper. Mix well.

On a large platter toss the spinach with 1/4 cup of the vinaigrette. Arrange tuna, tomatoes, sliced fennel, artichoke hearts, olives and eggs on top. Drizzle the remaining vinaigrette on top. Season with more salt and pepper as desired.

Serves 6

Add some macaroni or orzo pasta to this salad and some crusty bread for a great lunch

Grilled Sweet Onions with Marinated Tomatoes & Black Pepper Vinaigrette with Goat Cheese

4 sweet onions
1/2 cup mirin
1 tablespoon brown sugar
1 teaspoon minced ginger
4 vine-ripened tomatoes
2 teaspoons minced garlic
2 teaspoons chopped basil
4 tablespoons olive oil

BLACK PEPPER
VINAIGRETTE
2 tablespoons balsamic vinegar
1/2 teaspoon freshly ground black pepper
2 tablespoons sugar
2 tablespoons water
1/2 cup olive oil
Salt to taste
Mixed greens
5 ounces crumbled goat cheese

Slice the onions thinly. Blend together mirin, brown sugar and ginger. Pour over the onions to marinate. Grill the onions until soft.

Cut the tomatoes into 1/4 inch slices. Blend the garlic, ginger, basil and olive oil together and pour over tomatoes to marinate.

Mix all of the vinaigrette ingredients in a bowl until emulsified. Pour over the onions and tomatoes.

Place some of the greens on the plate. Top with the onions and tomatoes and crumbled goat cheese.

Serves 6

You will find mirin in the Asian section of most markets. If not, substitue rice-wine vinegar.

Crusty Pizza Bread
with Gorgonzola Caesar Salad

1 tablespoon white wine vinegar
2 tablespoons freshly
squeezed lemon juice
1 1/2 teaspoons minced garlic
1 egg yolk
1 tablespoon Dijon mustard
Dash Worcestershire sauce
6 anchovy fillets
Pinch freshly ground pepper
1/2 cup olive oil
1/4 cup crumbled Gorgonzola cheese
2 tablespoons freshly
grated Parmesan cheese

About 2 heads torn romaine lettuce
1 ball of fresh purchased pizza dough
Flour for dusting work surface
1/2 cup roasted garlic paste
1 tablespoon finely chopped fresh thyme
6 tablespoons freshly grated Parmesan
cheese, plus extra for garnish
Coarse cornmeal for
sprinkling on baking sheets
Crumbled gorgonzola cheese for garnish

For the dressing: Put the vinegar, lemon juice, garlic, egg yolk, mustard, Worcestershire sauce, anchovies, and pepper in a blender and blend until well mixed. With the machine running, add the olive oil, at first by drops and then as the mixture emulsifies, in a thick steady stream until all the oil is incorporated. Pulse in the gorgonzola to taste and the parmesan. Scrape into a bowl, cover, and refrigerate until needed. You should have about 1 1/3 cups. (The dressing keeps, refrigerated, for 2 to 3 days.)

Place 2 large baking sheets in the oven and preheat to 500 degrees. May use a pizza stone if you have one. Put the romaine in a bowl and pour the dressing over all and toss well.

Divide the dough into 6 equal balls. Working on a surface free of flour, roll each ball under your palm. As it rolls, it will stick slightly to the surface, creating tension that helps form a tight, round ball. Dust the work surface lightly with the flour, pat each ball down lightly, dust the tops with flour, cover with a towel and let rise again for about 15 minutes.

With a rolling pin, roll each ball into a circle 8 or 9 inches in diameter and about 1/8 inch thick. Brush each round with a generous tablespoon of the garlic paste and sprinkle with 1/2 teaspoon of the thyme and 1 tablespoon of the parmesan.

Remove the baking sheets from the oven, sprinkle evenly with cornmeal, and transfer the rounds to the sheets. Bake until slightly underdone (they should be lightly browned around the edges, but still pliable), 8 to 12 minutes. Let the crusts cool very briefly before filling.

Transfer the crusts to plates, top with a large handful of salad, and sprinkle with a small amount of gorgonzola and parmesan cheese. Serve open face.

NOTE: This dish is excellent with grilled fish or shrimp added to the salad.

Pizza dough is available in many specialty stores for about $1.00. It is easy to work with as long as you remember to remove it from the refrigerator, and let it rest for about 45 minutes. It will relax and then form beautifully into rounds for baking.

Serves 6

Cream of Asparagus Soup

1 1/2 pounds asparagus stalks,
save tips for garnish
3 medium leeks, white part only
3 tablespoons butter
1 1/2 quarts chicken stock
Salt
2 tablespoons cornstarch
3 tablespoons heavy cream
Fresh chervil sprigs

Peel, wash and drain the asparagus and cut each stalk into 3 or 4 pieces. Slice, wash and drain the leeks.

Melt the butter in a saucepan; add the leeks, cover the pan, and cook over low heat for 8 minutes. Be sure they do not brown. When the leeks are tender, add the asparagus and cover the pan again. Cook until the vegetables have rendered all their liquid and this has reduced completely, about 15 minutes.

Add the chicken stock and a little salt, bring to a boil, and simmer for 15 minutes.

Put the cornstarch in a small bowl, add a little cold water, and mix well. Add to the soup, stirring constantly; let it boil briefly until thickened, then puree in a food processor or blender. Strain through a fine sieve to remove any remaining fibers.

Return the soup to the saucepan and bring it back to a boil. Add the cream and immediately remove the pan from the heat.

Check for seasoning, garnish with chervil sprigs and asparagus tips, and serve hot, either in a tureen or in individual bowls.

RATATOUILLE

1 small zucchini
1 small yellow squash
1 small red bell pepper
1 small yellow bell pepper
1 small green bell pepper
3 tablespoons olive oil
1 small red onion, chopped fine
1 medium tomato, seeded and pureed
2 teaspoons minced garlic
3 tablespoons finely chopped
fresh parsley leaves
2 tablespoons finely chopped
fresh basil leaves
1 tablespoon finely chopped
fresh thyme leaves

12 ounces soft mild goat cheese
at room temp
Mixed baby greens
Red and yellow cherry tomatoes, halved

PESTO VINAIGRETTE

3/4 cup packed fresh basil leaves
1/2 tablespoon minced garlic
1/2 tablespoon minced shallot
1 tablespoon freshly grated Parmesan
1 tablespoon pine nuts, toasted golden
1 1/2 tablespoons white wine vinegar
1/2 cup plus 2 tablespoons olive oil

Ratatouille & Goat Cheese Salad with Pesto Vinaigrette

In a blender blend all vinaigrette ingredients with salt and pepper to taste until smooth.

Cut eggplant, zucchini, yellow squash and bell peppers into 1/4-inch dice. In a large heavy skillet cook eggplant in 1 tablespoon oil over moderate heat, stirring until tender and transfer to a bowl. In a skillet cook zucchini, yellow squash and onion with salt and pepper to taste in 1 tablespoon oil over moderate heat, stirring, until crisp-tender, 3 to 5 minutes, and transfer to bowl. Cook bell peppers in remaining tablespoon oil in same manner and transfer to bowl. Stir in tomato puree, garlic, herbs and salt and pepper to taste and cool ratatouille completely.

Preheat the oven to 375 degrees. Grease a 9-inch round springform pan or baking dish.

Fill the springform pan with the ratatouille. Cut the goat cheese into rounds and place on top of the ratatouille. Bake in the oven for 10 minutes, or until heated through.

In a large bowl toss the greens with 1/4 cup vinaigrette and divide among 8 plates.

Cut the ratatouille into wedges or squares and place in the center of each plate. Drizzle each salad with more of the vinaigrette and garnish with tomatoes.

Serves 6

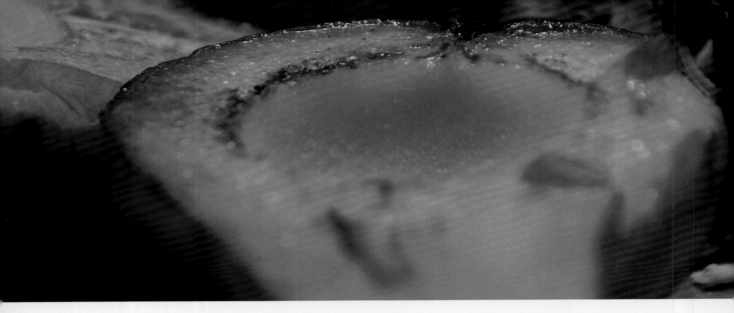

3/4 cup blanched hazelnuts
1/4 cup plus 1 teaspoon hazelnut oil
1/2 cup plus 2 tablespoons olive oil
4 Comice or Bartlett pears,
peeled, cored and cut into eighths
4 tablespoons unsalted butter
2 teaspoons thyme leaves
1 tablespoon finely diced shallot plus 2
tablespoons thinly diced shallot
2 1/2 tablespoons sherry vinegar
2 tablespoons rice vinegar
6 heads Belgian endive,
core removed, separated into spears
One package arugula, cleaned and dried
1/4 pound triple-cream cow's
milk blue cheese (St. Agur)
Salt and freshly ground black pepper

Sautéing the pears releases the sugar and they become beautifully caramelized. Serve this salad with a pork loin roast.

Roasted Pear Salad with Endive, Hazelnuts & Blue Cheese

Preheat the oven to 375 degrees. Toast the hazelnuts on a baking sheet or on top of the oven in a non-stick skillet until they smell nutty and are a light golden brown. Remove and toss with 1 teaspoon hazelnut oil and a healthy pinch of salt. When they have cooled, chop the nuts coarsely.

Heat two large sauté pans over high heat for 2 minutes. Swirl 1 tablespoon olive oil into each pan, and then carefully place the pears in the pan, cut side down. Add 2 tablespoons butter to each pan and season each batch with 1 teaspoon salt and 1 teaspoon thyme.

Reduce the heat to medium-high and cook the pears about 6 minutes, until they're golden brown on the first side. Carefully turn the pears over and cook another 3 to 4 minutes, until the second side is golden brown and the pears are tender but not mushy.

Using the large chef's knife pound or mash six of the pear wedges to a chunky paste. Combine the diced shallot, sherry vinegar, rice vinegar and 3/4 teaspoon salt in a medium bowl, and let sit for 5 minutes.

Whisk in the remaining 1/4 cup hazelnut oil and 1/2 cup olive oil. Stir in the pear puree and taste for balance and seasoning.

Place the remaining roasted pear wedges, the endive and the sliced shallots in a large salad bowl, and toss with about three-quarters of the vinaigrette. Season with 1/4 teaspoon salt and a few grindings of black pepper, and toss gently, being careful not to break up the pears.

Toss in the arugula gently and taste for seasoning, adding more vinaigrette if you like.

Arrange half the salad on a large platter. Use a vegetable peeler to make long ribbons of the blue cheese and place half of them in around the greens. Sprinkle half of the nuts on top. Place the remaining salad on top, and finish with shavings of cheese and the rest of the nuts.

Serves 6

Pork Tenderloin Salad
with Caramelized Onion Dressing

1 pork tenderloin
1/4 head red cabbage, shredded
3 sprigs of fresh thyme
1 head Boston lettuce,
torn into bite size pieces
1/2 red pepper, julienne

DRESSING
2 yellow onions, cut into dice
1 tablespoon olive oil
1 teaspoon sugar
1/4 cup Balsamic vinegar
3/4 cup olive oil

Sear the pork tenderloin in a dry sauté pan. Transfer to a 400 degree oven and roast in the oven for 25 minutes.

Cook the onions in olive oil on a low heat until translucent and caramelized, about 30 minutes.

Add the onions to the vinegar and slowly add the olive oil.

Toss half of the dressing with cabbage, lettuce, thyme and red pepper.

Slice the pork tenderloin and arrange on top of the salad ingredients. Pour the remainder of the dressing over the top of the pork tenderloin.

Serves 4

Serve this salad with roasted sweet potato fries. Cut the sweet potatoes into wedges, toss with olive oil, salt and pepper and roast in a 400 degree oven for 45 minutes.

Thai Flank Steak Salad

DRESSING
1/3 cup fresh lime juice
1 1/2 tablespoons brown sugar
1 tablespoon grated peeled fresh ginger
1 tablespoon Thai fish sauce
1 to 2 teaspoons chile paste with garlic
1 flank steak, trimmed
1 tablespoon cracked black pepper

SALAD
3 cups mâche or baby greens
1 cup thinly sliced red cabbage
1 cup loosely packed fresh basil leaves
1 cup loosely packed fresh mint leaves
1/2 cup loosely packed fresh cilantro leaves
1/2 cup julienne-cut carrot
2 tablespoons finely chopped unsalted, dry-roasted peanuts

To prepare dressing, combine all of the ingredients in a bowl and stir well with a whisk.

Heat a large nonstick skillet or grill pan over medium-high heat. Rub both sides of steak with pepper. Add steak to pan, cook 6 minutes on each side or until desired degree of doneness. Remove from pan, place on a cutting board. Let stand 5 minutes. Cut steak diagonally across grain into thin slices. Place steak in a bowl. Drizzle with half of dressing and toss well.

Combine the mâche or greens, cabbage, basil, mint, cilantro and carrots in a large bowl. Drizzle with remaining dressing and toss well. Divide salad evenly among plates, arrange steak evenly over salad. Sprinkle each serving with some of the peanuts.

Serves 6

This salad has everything. It's crunchy and fresh with explosive flavors. If flank steak is not your favorite, substitute chicken or salmon. Watercress has a really nice peppery flavor, but can often be very woody. If you can find hydroponic watercress, it is delicious.

Spicy Cornbread Salad

1 pound cornbread, cut into cubes
1 cup halved cherry tomatoes
1 cup crumbled cotija cheese
1 cup cubed cucumber
1/4 cup finely chopped red onion
1 jalapeno chile, finely chopped
1/2 cup chopped fresh basil leaves
2/3 cup olive oil
2 lemons, zested and juiced
1 teaspoon salt
1 teaspoon freshly ground black pepper

Combine all the ingredients in a large bowl. Toss gently to combine. Place in a serving bowl and serve.

Serves 6

Cornbread is sold pre-made in most bakery sections of the market. I always check to make sure there is very little or no sugar. For added flavor I cut the cornbread into slices, spray with olive oil and grill. Its a bit smoky and crispy.

Grilled Pear Salad
with Bacon & Roquefort Vinaigrette

1 cup walnut halves, toasted
8 ounces sliced bacon
3 Bosc pears, sliced
Vegetable spray
8 cups mixed greens
1 cup crumbled Roquefort cheese
1/2 cup olive oil
1/4 cup walnut oil
1 tablespoon sherry vinegar
1 teaspoon Dijon mustard
Salt and freshly ground black pepper

Cook the bacon and crumble into small pieces. Set aside. Wipe out the pan and spray with vegetable spray. Sauté the pear slices until just tender and golden brown.

Place the salad greens in a large bowl. Mix together the sherry vinegar and the Dijon mustard. Gradually add the oils until emulsified. Season with salt and pepper. Toss with the greens until lightly coated.

To serve place the greens on a large platter. Arrange the pear slices on top and sprinkle the crumbled Roquefort cheese and bacon on top.

Serves 6

Sautéing the pear slices caramelizes them and they become really sweet. It is a great taste with the Roquefort cheese.

This salad is great for a Sunday night supper or for casual entertaining any time.

Spinach-Bacon Salad with Black Pepper Seared Filet Mignon & Caesar Dressing

CROUTONS

1/2 loaf country bread, crusts removed
1/2 cup finely grated Parmesan
1/4 cup olive oil
1 teaspoon paprika
1 garlic clove, minced
Sea salt and freshly ground
black pepper to taste

CAESAR DRESSING

1 egg yolk
6 anchovy fillets
2 tablespoons Dijon mustard
2 garlic cloves, peeled
2/3 cup olive oil
3/4 cup freshly grated Parmesan
1/4 cup freshly squeezed lemon juice

SALAD

1 1/2 pounds baby spinach
1 medium head radicchio
10 slices smoked bacon, crumbled
1 1/2 cups crumbled blue cheese
1/2 thinly sliced red onion
1 3-pound whole filet mignon

Preheat the oven to 350 degrees. Cut the bread into 1/2-inch cubes. You should have about 2 cups. Toss the bread with the Parmesan, olive oil, paprika, garlic and salt and pepper. Spread the bread cubes in a large pan. Bake, stirring once or twice, 10 to 15 minutes, or until golden brown. Let cool.

Place the egg into a food processor or blender. Add the anchovies, mustard and garlic. Process or blend until smooth. With the motor running, add the olive oil in a thin stream. Blend in the cheese and lemon juice. Season with salt and pepper.

Season the filet with black pepper. Drizzle with a little olive oil and sear in a very hot skillet. Place in a 400 degree oven for about 25 minutes. The filet should be medium-rare. Slice into thin slices.

Toss the spinach and radicchio with enough dressing to evenly coat the leaves. Scatter the croutons and crumbled bacon on top. Sprinkle with the cheese. Lay the filet mignon slices across the top of the salad.

Serves 6

Red Leaf Caesar Salad
with Parmesan Popovers

VINAIGRETTE

3 anchovy fillets
2 tablespoons fresh lemon juice
1 large garlic clove, minced
1 teaspoon Dijon mustard
1/2 teaspoon Worcestershire sauce
1/2 cup olive oil
Salt and pepper

POPOVERS

3 eggs
3/4 cup all-purpose flour
1/4 teaspoon salt
1/2 teaspoon freshly ground black pepper
1/2 teaspoon herbs de Provence
4 tablespoons chopped parsley leaves
1 cup whole milk
3/4 cup grated Parmesan

VINAIGRETTE

Place all of the ingredients for the vinaigrette in a blender except the olive oil. With the blender running, slowly add the olive oil. Season with salt and pepper. Toss the salad with the vinaigrette and serve with the Parmesan popovers.

PARMESAN POPOVERS
(MAKES 8)

Preheat the oven to 400 degrees.

In a blender, combine the eggs, flour, salt, pepper and herbs, milk and cheese. Blend on medium speed.

Spray a mini-muffin pan with nonstick cooking spray. Pour the batter into the muffin cups filling each cup 3/4 cup full. Bake until puffed and golden brown, about 20 to 25 minutes. Remove the popovers from muffin tin and cool on a wire rack.

Serves 6

The secret to great popovers is to make the batter and refrigerate it for at least one hour or overnight. If you preheat the muffin tin before placing the batter into it they will puff up even more.

Silky Sautéed Red Peppers
with Grilled Bread & Arugula

6 red bell peppers
1/2 cup plus 3 tablespoons
balsamic vinegar
1 teaspoon sea salt, or to taste
1/4 cup olive oil
8 cups arugula
Tuscan bread

Wash the peppers, quarter them lengthwise, and remove and discard the seeds and membranes. Place in a very large skillet and toss with the 1/2 cup vinegar and the salt. Cover and cook over low heat until soft and tender, about 25 minutes. Toss from time to time, adjusting the heat so the peppers cook slowly. By the end of the cooking time, most of the liquid will have evaporated. Do not increase the heat to speed up cooking, or the peppers will scorch and toughen.

Once the peppers have softened, transfer them to a large platter. Return the skillet to the heat, increase the heat to medium, and deglaze with the final 3 tablespoons vinegar, using a spatula to completely remove any flavorful bits that may have stuck to the pan.

Add the oil and heat just until warmed through, less than 1 minute. Pour the liquid over the peppers, toss, and taste for seasoning. Cool for at least 30 minutes before serving at room temperature. As they cool, the peppers will continue to soften and to absorb the oil and vinegar, giving them a complex subtle flavor.

Slice the bread, brush with olive oil and grill. Serve with the peppers next to a handful of arugula that has been tossed with a little olive oil and salt and pepper.

Serves 6

Romaine Wedges with Blue Cheese Vinaigrette

1/2 cup olive oil
3 tablespoons balsamic vinegar
1 1/2 teaspoons anchovy paste
1 garlic clove, minced
1 cup crumbled blue cheese
Hearts of romaine, halved lengthwise
1/2 small red onion, thinly sliced

Combine the olive oil, vinegar, anchovy paste and garlic in a medium bowl to blend. Whisk in the cheese, leaving some to garnish.

Season with salt and cracked black pepper.

Place romaine wedges on plates.

Drizzle the dressing over the center of each and top with onion and remaining cheese.

Serves 6

Most men love a good wedge salad. It is simple and pairs well with a nice steak. For added flavor try grilling the wedges of romaine.

CROQUETTES

12 ounces cream cheese,
room temperature
6 ounces thinly sliced
smoked salmon, chopped
2 tablespoons chopped fresh dill
1/4 teaspoon white pepper
1/2 teaspoon Tabasco
1/2 cup all-purpose flour
1 large egg, beaten to blend
2 cups bread crumbs (Panko)
Oil for frying
6 baby greens

VINAIGRETTE

1 small bunch cleaned
and stemmed watercress
1 tablespoon minced shallot
1 garlic clove, minced
1 tablespoon white wine vinegar
Juice of one lemon
1/2 cup olive oil
Salt and pepper to taste

Smoked Salmon Croquettes on Baby Greens with Watercress Vinaigrette

For the croquettes: Blend cream cheese and smoked salmon in a a food processor until almost smooth, with small salmon bits remaining. Mix in dill, white pepper and Tabasco. Drop salmon mixture by generous tablespoons onto large baking sheet. Refrigerate until firm, about 30 minutes.

Place flour in a small bowl. Dip 1 mound of salmon mixture into flour, coating completely (shake off excess). Using hands, roll mixture into a ball. Dip into beaten egg, then bread crumbs, coating completely. Return to baking sheet. Repeat with remaining salmon mixture, flour, egg and bread crumbs. Cover and refrigerate croquettes until cold, about 20 minutes.

Add enough oil (canola oil) to large saucepan to reach depth of 3 inches. Heat to 350 degrees. Working in batches, fry croquettes until golden brown, about 2 minutes. Using tongs, transfer to paper towels; drain.

Make the vinaigrette: In a blender place cleaned watercress, shallot, garlic, vinegar and lemon juice. Puree until smooth. Slowly add olive oil in a stream until emulsified. Add salt and pepper to taste.

Toss the greens with the vinaigrette. Mound some of the greens on the plate and place 2 croquettes on top. Garnish with a lemon wedge.

Serves 6

2 teaspoons balsamic vinegar
2 teaspoons roasted garlic
1 teaspoon chopped fresh rosemary
2 teaspoons chopped fresh sage
1/4 cup olive oil
1 1/2 pounds stemmed and
trimmed portabello mushrooms
Salt and freshly ground pepper
4 cups mixed greens
Mustard Seed Vinaigrette
Parmesan Chips

MUSTARD SEED VINAIGRETTE

1 tablespoon Dijon mustard
2 teaspoons toasted mustard seed
2 tablespoons seasoned rice wine vinegar
2 tablespoons fresh orange juice
2 teaspoons chopped fresh dill
1/4 cup olive oil
Salt and pepper to taste

PARMESAN CHIPS

Vegetable spray
1 cup freshly and finely grated Parmesan
cheese or aged Asiago cheese

Grilled Portabello Mushrooms
on Savory Greens with Parmesan Chips

Prepare a charcoal fire or preheat a stovetop grill. In a medium bowl, whisk together the vinegar, roasted garlic, rosemary, sage and oil. Brush the mushrooms liberally with the mixture. Season with salt and pepper.

Grill the mushrooms over moderate heat, until just softened, turning once or twice. To serve, arrange the greens on individual plates. Lightly drizzle with the vinaigrette. Slice the mushrooms thickly and arrange on the greens. Surround with the Parmesan chips and serve immediately.

MUSTARD SEED VINAIGRETTE
In a small bowl whisk all the ingredients until combined.

PARMESAN CHIPS
Preheat the oven to 350 degrees. Line a baking sheet with parchment paper. Lightly spray the paper with vegetable spray. Sprinkle the cheese into thin 3-inch rounds, 4 inches apart. Bake until the cheese melts and the chips begin to brown, 5-10 minutes. Using a metal spatula, carefully remove each chip and place on a rack or drape over a rolling pin to form curls. Cool. The chips should be used within a few hours.

Serves 6

The Parmesan chips can be made in the oven or in a small non-stick skillet. They are great on salads or floating on top of soup.

Lentils are readily available pre-cooked in vacuum sealed pouches. This certainly cuts down the prep time. Serve with grilled rack of lamb for a complete and easy dinner.

Spinach & Lentil Salad with Blue Cheese & Tart Cherry Vinaigrette

3/4 cup green lentils
7 tablespoons red-wine vinegar
8 slices bacon
1/4 cup olive oil
1/3 cup finely chopped shallot
1/4 cup water
1/2 cup dried unsweetened, tart cherries
2 tablespoons sugar
4 cups baby spinach leaves
1/3 cup blue cheese (about 2 ounces)

In a heavy saucepan cover lentils with water by 2 inches and simmer until just tender but not falling apart, about 15 minutes. Drain lentils well in a sieve. Rinse under cold water and drain well.

In a bowl toss lentils with 2 tablespoons vinegar and salt and pepper to taste. Lentils may be made 2 days ahead and chilled, covered. Bring to room temperature before proceeding.

In a skillet cook bacon over moderate heat until crisp. Transfer to paper towels to drain. Crumble bacon.

In a saucepan heat 2 tablespoons oil over moderate heat until hot and cook shallot, stirring until gold brown. Stir in water, cherries, sugar and remaining 5 tablespoons vinegar and simmer, stirring occasionally, until liquid is reduced by about half, about 10 minutes. Reduce heat to low and whisk in remaining 2 tablespoons oil in a slow stream until emulsified. Season vinaigrette with salt and pepper.

Add half of the vinaigrette to lentils and toss well. In another bowl toss spinach with half of lentil mixture, half of bacon, half of cheese, remaining vinaigrette, and salt and pepper to taste.

Divide remaining lentil mixture among plates and top with spinach mixture. Sprinkle salads with remaining bacon and cheese.

Yellow Rice Salad with Roasted Peppers & Spicy Black Beans

4 teaspoons ground cumin
1/2 cup fresh lime juice
2 1/2 tablespoons vegetable oil
1/2 teaspoon tumeric
2 cups water
1 cup basmati rice
1 teaspoon salt
1/2 cup thinly sliced green onions
1 (15-ounce) can black beans, rinsed, drained
1/2 cup chopped roasted red peppers from jar
1/2 cup chopped green bell pepper
1/3 cup chopped fresh cilantro
1 1/2 teaspoons minced chipotle chiles

Stir 3 teaspoons cumin in small dry skillet over medium heat just until fragrant, about 1 minute. Remove from heat. Whisk lime juice and oil into skillet.

Stir tumeric and remaining cumin in heavy medium saucepan over medium heat until fragrant, about 1 minute. Add 2 cups water, rice and salt; bring to boil. Reduce heat to low and cover, simmer until water is absorbed, about 15 minutes. Cool rice. Mix onions and half of dressing into rice. Season with salt and pepper.

Combine black beans, all peppers, cilantro, chipotle chiles and remaining dressing in medium bowl. Toss to coat. Season with salt and pepper.

Mound bean mixture in center of platter. Surround with rice salad.

Serves 6

I often mix the beans and rice salad together. The colors are great. These flavors work well with grilled pork tenderloin or chicken.

Spring

Edamame and Pea Salad with Grilled Onions & Goat Cheese

1/4 cup olive oil
1/4 pound sliced bacon, cut into 1/4-inch dice
1 Vidalia onion, cut into 1/2-inch wedges through the root end
1 large garlic clove, thinly sliced 1 cup frozen, shelled edamame, thawed
1 1/2 cups frozen peas, thawed
2 cups sugar snap peas
3 tablespoons fresh lemon juice
1 teaspoon Dijon mustard
2 teaspoons coarsely chopped mint
Salt and freshly ground pepper
2 ounces aged goat cheese, crumbled (1/2 cup)

All of the ingredients in this salad compliment each other beautifully. It works well as a side dish with grilled pork tenderloin.

In a large skillet, heat 1 teaspoon of the olive oil. Add the bacon and cook over moderate heat, stirring occasionally, until crisp, about 5 minutes. Transfer the bacon to a plate. Add the onion wedges to the skillet and cook, turning occasionally, until golden, 2 minutes. Transfer the onions and garlic to a plate.

Meanwhile, bring a large saucepan of salted water to a boil. Add the edamame, peas and sugar snap peas and cook until the sugar snaps are crisp-tender, about 4 minutes.

Drain and cool under running water. Pat dry.

In a large bowl, mix the lemon juice with the mustard and the remaining 3 tablespoons plus 2 teaspoons of olive oil. Add the edamame, peas, sugar snaps, bacon, onion wedges, garlic and mint. Season the salad with salt and pepper and toss until combined.

Sprinkle the goat cheese over the salad and serve at room temperature.

Servees 6

Asparagus with Lemon-Mustard Sauce

1 1/2 pounds asparagus,
peeled and trimmed
1 tablespoon Dijon mustard
1/2 teaspoon salt
1/4 teaspoon freshly ground black pepper
2 teaspoons lemon juice
4 tablespoons virgin olive oil
24 Niçoise olives
2 tablespoons drained capers
1 ripe tomato, seeded and cut into pieces
1/4 cup flat-leaf parsley leaves

Place the asparagus in the bottom of a saucepan and add enough water to cover. Bring to a boil and cook for about 5 minutes. Remove and spread out on a platter to cool.

Combine the sauce ingredients in a small bowl.

Arrange the asparagus on a platter and spoon the lemon-mustard sauce over the spears. Sprinkle with the parsley leaves and serve.

Serves 6

This is my standby salad at Easter. Whether serving ham, salmon or lamb it works well. Make it ahead. It looks great on the buffet table.

Spaghetti Salad with Sugar Snap Peas & Red Peppers

1/2 pound thin spaghetti
1 pound sugar snap peas
1 cup vegetable oil
1/4 cup rice vinegar
1/3 cup soy sauce
3 tablespoons dark sesame oil
1 tablespoon honey
2 garlic cloves, minced
1 teaspoon grated fresh ginger
2 tablespoons white sesame seeds, toasted
1 1/2 teaspoon salt
1 teaspoon freshly ground black pepper
2 red bell peppers, cored, seeded and thinly sliced
4 scallions, sliced diagonally
1 tablespoon white sesame seeds, toasted
3 tablespoons chopped fresh parsley leaves

Bring a large pot of salted water to a boil. Add the spaghetti and cook according to package directions. Drain and set aside.

Meanwhile, bring another large pot of salted water to a boil, add the sugar snap peas, return to a boil, and cook for 3 minutes, until crisp tender. Lift the peas from the water with a slotted spoon and immerse them in a bowl of ice water. Drain.

For the dressing, whisk together the vegetable oil, rice vinegar, soy sauce, sesame oil, honey, garlic, ginger, 1 tablespoon sesame seeds, peanut butter, salt to taste and the pepper in a medium bowl.

Combine the spaghetti, sugar snap peas, peppers and scallions in a large bowl. Pour the dressing over the spaghetti mixture. Add the scallions and the parsley and mix again. Sprinkle with toasted sesame seeds.

Serves 6

I love this salad served with grilled salmon. The colors and flavors are fantastic together.

Butter Lettuce with Cucumber Ranch Dressing & Cherry Tomatoes

2 heads butter or Boston Lettuce
1 box cherry or grape tomatoes

CUCUMBER RANCH DRESSING
Makes 2 1/4 cups
1 medium cucumber, peeled, halved lengthwise, seeded, and grated on the large holes of a box grater
1 tablespoon finely chopped shallot
1/4 cup sour cream
1/4 cup low-fat buttermilk
1/4 cup mayonnaise
3 1/2 tablespoons fresh lemon juice (about 1 lemon)
1 1/4 teaspoons sea salt
Pinch of cayenne pepper
3 tablespoons finely chopped fresh flat-leaf parsley
3 tablespoons finely chopped fresh chives

Stir together cucumber, shallot, sour cream, buttermilk, mayonnaise, lemon juice, salt, cayenne, parsley and chives in a medium bowl. Season with additional salt and cayenne, if desired. Dressing can be refrigerated in an airtight container for up to 3 days.

Tear the leaves of the lettuce and add to a bowl with the tomatoes. Add about 1/2 cup of the dressing until all of the leaves are lightly coated.

Serves 6

Adding cucumber gives this dressing a very fresh, clean flavor. There are so many varieties of small tomatoes. Try them all.

Charleston Place Crab Cakes

1 cup mayonnaise
1 egg white
3 tablespoons lemon juice
2 teaspoons dry mustard
2 teaspoons Old Bay Seasoning
1/2 teaspoon cayenne
Pinch salt and pepper
1 pound crab meat, lump
1/2 cup fine cracker meal
2 cups fresh bread crumbs
3 tablespoons clarified butter
2 tablespoons olive oil

Mix thoroughly together the mayonnaise, egg white, lemon juice, dry mustard, Old Bay Seasoning, cayenne and the salt and pepper. Pick through the crab meat for tiny shell pieces and then fold crab meat into mixture with a rubber spatula. Add the cracker meal by folding in gently.

Make fresh bread crumbs by taking 6-8 pieces of regular white bread and remove the crust. Process in a food processor for approximately one minute. Mix the bread crumbs into crab mixture. Form into cakes and refrigerate for 30 minutes. When ready, sauté on each side 2-3 minutes in a clarified butter and olive oil. Serve immediately with honey mustard sauce.

Serves 6

A few years ago I took a group to Charleston for a 4 day "Salute to Southern Chefs." Chef Robert Wagner at Charleston Place shared this recipe with us for his crab cakes. They are amazing. The key ingredient is fresh bread crumbs. Don't skip that part!

Salad of Grilled Portabellos, Asparagus & Sweet Peas

Color, texture, flavor. This salad has it all.
The presentation is exciting and goes well with grilled chicken or steak.

16-20 asparagus spears,
trimmed and peeled
2/3 cup fresh peas
8-12 thick slices portabello mushrooms
3 tablespoons olive oil
Salt and freshly ground black pepper
3, 3/4-inch thick slices country-style bread,
cut in half on the diagonal
1 bunch of arugula, washed and dried
1 bunch watercress, washed and dried
1 teaspoon chopped shallots
2 tablespoons dry white wine
3 tablespoons unsalted butter,
at room temperature
1 teaspoon chopped flat-leaf parsley
1 teaspoon chopped fresh tarragon
2 tablespoons fresh lemon juice

Pour about 1 inch of water into a deep skillet and bring to a boil over high heat. Add the asparagus and cook for about 1 minute, until crisp-tender. Remove with a slotted spoon or tongs and drain on paper towels. Add the peas to the boiling water and cook for about 1 minute, until crisp-tender. Drain and set aside.

Prepare a charcoal, gas, or stove-top grill.

Brush the mushrooms and asparagus with 2 tablespoons of the olive oil and season with salt and pepper. Grill for 3-4 minutes, until the asparagus just begins to color and the mushrooms soften slightly. Transfer to a plate and set aside. Grill the bread for about 1 minute a side, until lighly toasted.

Arrange the arugula and cress on serving plates and top with the grilled bread. Arrange the mushrooms and asparagus on the bread, spooning any accumulated juices over the greens.

In a small sauté pan, heat the remaining 1 tablespoon oil over medium heat. Add the shallots and wine and cook, stirring, for about 1 minute. Remove from the heat and whisk in the butter a tablespoon at a time. Stir in the peas, parsley, tarragon and lemon juice. Return the pan to low heat and cook, stirring gently, for about 1 minute to warm the peas. Season with salt and pepper and spoon over the salads.

Serves 6

Asparagus Ribbons
with Lemon & Goat Cheese

1 pound large asparagus spears, trimmed
1 1/2 cups cherry tomatoes, halved
2 tablespoons finely chopped fresh chives
2 tablespoons fresh lemon juice
2 teaspoons olive oil
1/2 teaspoon freshly ground black pepper
1/2 teaspoon Dijon mustard
1/4 teaspoon sugar
1/4 teaspoon salt
1/2 cup crumbled goat cheese

Hold each asparagus spear by the tip end. Shave asparagus into ribbons with a vegetable peeler to measure 3 cups. Reserve asparagus tips for another use. Combine asparagus and tomatoes in a medium bowl.

Combine the chives, lemon juice, olive oil, pepper, Dijon, sugar and salt, stirring with a whisk. Drizzle over the asparagus mixture, tossing gently to coat.

Top with goat cheese.

Serves 6

This is a great salad for spring. The asparagus is crisp and delicious. Poach the asparagus tips and toss with fettuccini. Mix together the zest and juice of 2 lemons, 1/3 cup of olive oil, 1/4 cup chopped parsley, salt and pepper and you have a great side dish. Top with the goat cheese.

The panko-crusted goat cheese may also be baked on a parchment lined baking sheet for 10 minutes at 400 degrees.

Panko-Crusted Goat Cheese with Tomato-Asparagus Salad

1/2 pound asparagus, peeled and cut into
2-inch pieces on the diagonal
One 11-ounce log of mild goat cheese
1/2 cup all-purpose flour
2 eggs, slightly beaten
1 cup panko
1/2 cup vegetable oil
8 cups baby arugula
3 small ripe tomatoes, sliced

BALSAMIC VINAIGRETTE
2 garlic cloves, thinly sliced
1/2 cup olive oil
3 tablespoons balsamic vinegar
1 teaspoon salt
Freshly cracked black pepper

Blanch the asparagus pieces by immersing them in a small saucepan of boiling water for 1 minute. Plunge the drained pieces into a bowl of cold water and allow to chill. The asparagus can be prepared in advance and refrigerated.

Slice the goat cheese into 8 pieces, dipping the knife into hot water between cuts to make neat slices. Set them on a plate.

Use 3 separate bowls to hold the flour, eggs and panko. Coat the goat cheese in the flour and shake off any excess flour. Dip each slice into the eggs and then into the panko. Gently place each slice on a plate. Refrigerate until ready to fry.

Heat the oil in a nonstick skillet over medium heat. Add the slices to the hot oil and fry until lightly browned, about 2 minutes. Turn and brown the other side. Remove the slices and drain on a stack of paper towels.

Divide the arugula among plates. Top each with 2 tomato slices and some asparagus pieces. Spoon the vinaigrette, including the garlic slivers, over all. Place a piece of the warm goat cheese on top of the vegetables.

Combine the garlic and oil in a small bowl. Whisk in the remaining ingredients for the vinaigrette.

Serves 6

Main course salads are great for luncheons or an early supper. Warm crusty bread and a crisp fruity sauvignon blanc are the perfect combination.

Poached Salmon Salad with Warm Potatoes, Red Chile Deviled Eggs & Smoked Chile Dressing

1 tablespoon black peppercorns
Salt
2 tablespoons fresh lemon juice
12 sprigs fresh flat-leaf parsley
1 1/2 pounds salmon fillet
1/4 cup Kalamata olives, pitted
and coarsely chopped
3 green onions, white
and green parts, thinly sliced
1 tablespoon capers
3 tablespoons finely
chopped fresh cilantro
3 medium red potatoes (about 1 pound)

Red Chile Deviled Eggs (next page)
Smoked Chile Dressing
(see Dressings section)

Combine 4 cups of water, 1 tablespoon of salt, the peppercorns, lemon juice and parsley in a 9-inch high-sided sauté pan or shallow pot and bring to a simmer over medium heat. Place the salmon in the pan, cover and simmer until just cooked through, about 10 minutes. Remove with a slotted spoon to a plate and cool slightly.

Using a fork, flake the salmon into bite-sized pieces and place in a large bowl.

Fold in the olives, green onions, capers, chopped cilantro and 1/2 cup of the smoked chile dressing and stir until combined; season with salt. Cover and refrigerate for at least 30 minutes and up to 1 day before serving.

Put the potatoes in a medium saucepan of salted cold water and bring to a boil over high heat. Cook until tender when pierced with a knife, 12 to 15 minutes. Drain, set aside to cool slightly and slice 1/4 inch thick.

To serve, mound the salad in the center of dinner plates. Arrange the potato slices and deviled eggs around the perimeter of the plates and drizzle everything with the remaining 1/2 cup dressing.

Red Chile Deviled Eggs

6 large eggs
1/4 cup prepared mayonnaise
2 teaspoons chipotle chile purée
2 teaspoons ancho chile powder,
plus extra for garnish
2 tablespoons finely chopped fresh chives
2 tablespoons finely
chopped fresh cilantro
Salt and freshly ground black pepper

Put the eggs in a medium saucepan and add enough cold water to cover them by 1 inch. Bring just to a boil over high heat, then turn off the heat, cover the pot, and let sit for 15 minutes.

Drain the eggs and run under cold water to cool. Remove the shell from each egg. Slice each egg in half lengthwise and carefully remove the yolk. Place the yolks in a medium bowl and mash with a fork. Add the mayonnaise, chipotle purée, ancho powder, chives and cilantro and stir until combined; season with salt and pepper.

Carefully spoon the mixture back into the egg white halves. These can be made up to 8 hours in advance. Dust with ancho powder before serving.

Chile-Lime Crab Salad with Tomato & Avocado

5 tablespoons fresh lime juice
6 tablespoons olive oil
1 tablespoon very finely
chopped jalapeno
1 tablespoon chopped cilantro,
plus cilantro leaves for garnish
1/2 tablespoon honey
1/2 teaspoon minced garlic
Salt and freshly ground
black pepper
1 pound lump crabmeat
2 avocados, diced
1/3 cup minced red onion
2 large heirloom tomatoes cut into
1/2-inch thick slices
Tortilla chips, for serving

In a small bowl, combine the lime juice with the olive oil, jalapeno, chopped cilantro, honey and garlic. Season with salt and pepper.

In a small bowl, toss the crab with 3 tablespoons of the dressing and season with salt and pepper. In a medium bowl, gently toss the avocado with the red onion and 2 tablespoons of the dressing; season with salt and pepper.

Place a tomato slice on each plate and season with salt. Top with the avocado and the crab and garnish with the cilantro. Drizzle the remaining dressing on top and serve with the tortilla chips.

Canned super lump crabmeat is a great alternative to expensive fresh crab. It is delicious in salad, pasta and crab cakes.

Grilling the avocados gives them a smoky taste and they stay a vibrant green. The taste and color really compliment the coleslaw.

Coleslaw with Grilled Avocados

1/2 cup mayonnaise

1/3 cup olive oil

1/3 cup fresh lime juice
(about 2 large limes)

1/4 cup red wine vinegar

2 ears corn, husked, desilked, blanched in
boiling water for 2 minutes, drained and
kernels cut off the cob (about 1 cup)

2 tablespoons sugar

2 tablespoons catsup

A few dashes Tabasco sauce

Salt and freshly cracked
black pepper to taste

2 cups shredded green cabbage

1 cup shredded red cabbage

1 cup shredded carrots
(about 1 medium carrot)

3 ripe but firm avocados,
halved and pitted but not peeled

2 tablespoons olive oil

1 tablespoon chili powder

1 tablespoon ground cumin

To make the dressing: In a food processor or blender, combine all the ingredients and purée until smooth.

In a medium bowl, combine the green and red cabbage and the carrots. Add the dressing, mix well. Cover and refrigerate.

Sprinkle the avocados with the olive oil, chili powder, cumin and salt and pepper to taste. Place them on the grill over a medium-hot fire, cut side down, and cook for 3 to 5 minutes, or until seared, really seared. Pull the avocados off the grill and, as soon as they are cool enough to handle, turn them out of their skins, slice them, and serve on top of generous helpings of the slaw. (If the avocadoes don't slip out of their skins easily, just spoon out chunks on top of the slaw).

Serves 6

Grilled Asparagus Panzanella

6 (1-inch) slices country
style bread or ciabatta
1/4 cup red wine vinegar
2 cloves garlic; finely chopped
Salt and freshly ground black pepper
1/2 cup olive oil
1 1/2 pounds grilled asparagus,
cut into 1-inch pieces
16-20 red and yellow
cherry tomatoes, quartered
1 small red onion, halved and thinly sliced
1/2 cup Niçoise olives
2 tablespoons capers, drained
8 fresh basil leaves, cut into thin ribbons,
plus more leaves for garnish

Heat the grill to high.

Grill the bread on both sides until slightly charred, about 1 minute per side. Remove from grill and cut each slice into 1-inch cubes. Grill the asparagus until charred. Cut into 1-inch pieces.

Whisk together the vinegar, garlic, 1/2 teaspoon salt, 1/4 teaspoon pepper, and the oil in a large bowl until combined.

Add the asparagus, red and yellow tomatoes, onion, olives, capers, grilled bread and basil and mix until combined. Season with salt and pepper.

Let sit at room temperature for at least 30 minutes and up to 1 hour before serving.

Serve on a large platter and garnish with basil leaves.

Serves 6

Sometimes I grill the bread at the last minute and then add to the salad. It retains the smoky flavor and stays crisp.

This salad has a great combination of color, crunch and variety of flavors.

Baby Greens with Blood Oranges
& Sage Prosciutto Polenta Croutons

SAGE PROSCIUTTO CROUTONS

2 teaspoons virgin olive oil
1 ounce prosciutto, finely diced
2 cloves garlic, minced
7 fresh sage leaves, finely chopped
1 cup chicken stock
1 cup water
1/2 teaspoon coarse sea salt
1/2 cup polenta or coarsely
ground yellow cornmeal
Freshly ground black pepper
3 tablespoons freshly grated Parmesan
2 tablespoons butter
1/3 cup canola for frying

SALAD

6 cups baby greens
2 blood oranges, rind and pith removed
and cut into segments
3 tablespoons olive oil
1/2 teaspoon sea salt
Freshly ground black pepper
1 tablespoon white wine vinegar

To make the croutons: In a large heavy saucepan heat the olive oil over medium-low heat. Add the prosciutto, garlic and sage and sauté, stirring occasionally, until the prosciutto is crisp and the garlic is softened, about 4 minutes. Do not let the garlic burn. Transfer the mixture to a bowl and set aside.

Wipe the inside of the pan with a paper towel and return to the heat. Immediately add the chicken stock, water and salt and bring to a simmer over medium-high heat. When the liquid is simmering, gradually sprinkle the polenta over in a slow, thin stream, whisking constantly until all the grains have been incorporated and no lumps remain. Reduce the heat to low. Stir from time to time for about 20 minutes, or until the mixture pulls away from the sides of the pan. Add the prosciutto mixture and pepper to taste. Add the Parmesan and butter, stirring to mix evenly. The mixture will be very thick.

Serves 6

Zucchini Carpaccio

1/4 cup olive oil
2 tablespoons fresh lemon juice
Salt and freshly ground pepper
1 pound small green and yellow zucchini,
sliced 1/8-inch thick on
the diagonal with a mandoline
1 bunch arugula, large stems discarded
1 ounce Parmesan, shaved

In a medium bowl, whisk the olive oil with the lemon juice and season with salt and pepper. Add the zucchini and toss well; let stand for 3 minutes.

Arrange the zucchini slices, overlapping them slightly, on a platter.

Add the arugula to the bowl and toss with the dressing, then mound on the zucchini.

Scatter the Parmesan over the top and serve.

Serves 6

Italians love this simple raw salad. It is also great with asparagus.

1 cup fresh basil leaves
1/2 cup olive oil
1/2 cup white wine vinegar
1/4 cup honey
1 tablespoon Dijon mustard
1/3 cup heavy cream
Salt to taste
4 large tomatoes sliced 1/4-inch thick,
seasoned with salt
3/4 pound fresh mozzarella, thinly sliced
into 15 rounds

Blend the basil, oil, vinegar, honey and mustard for the dressing in a food processor or blender. With the motor running, add the cream and blend to emulsify; season with salt.

Assemble napoleons starting with a tomato slice, then a cheese slice, and some dressing. Alternate 3 more tomato slices and 2 more cheese slices, drizzling each layer with dressing.

Repeat with remaining tomatoes, cheese and dressing. Garnish with fresh basil leaves.

Serves 6

Insalata caprese is the most popular Italian salad. This elegant presentation becomes even more beautiful if heirloom tomatoes are available.

Asian Pesto Chicken Salad

2 tablespoons canola oil, if needed
1 box uncooked orzo
One purchased roasted chicken,
all of the meat removed
Salt and freshly ground
black pepper to taste
1 1/4 cups Asian Pesto,
plus additional for drizzling
1 pint cherry tomatoes, halved
Juice of 2 lemons
1/2 pound baby spinach

ASIAN PESTO
(Makes about 3 1/2 cups)
2 jalapeño chiles, stemmed and seeded
8 garlic cloves
1 tablespoon sugar
1 heaping tablespoon peeled
and minced fresh ginger
1 cup roasted salted macadamia nuts or
roasted salted peanuts
Zest of 2 lemons
2 cups olive oil
1 cup fresh basil leaves, packed
1 cup fresh mint leaves, packed
1/2 cup fresh cilantro leaves, packed

Bring a saucepan of lightly salted water to boil. Cook the orzo until just tender, about 10 minutes. Drain well.

In a large bowl, combine the chicken with 1 cup of the pesto, the orzo and the tomatoes. Season with salt and pepper. In a medium bowl, combine the remaining cup of pesto with the lemon juice, then toss with the spinach. Season with salt and pepper.

Divide the spinach mixture among plates. Mound the chicken salad on the spinach, drizzle with additional pesto, and serve.

ASIAN PESTO
In a blender or food processor, combine the chiles, garlic, sugar, ginger, nuts, zest and 1 cup of the oil and blend until smooth. Add the basil, mint, and cilantro and blend while slowly adding the remaining oil until a thick purée is formed. Season with salt and pepper. Store in a tightly covered jar and refrigerate.

Serves 6

Avocado & Hearts of Palm Salad with Bell Pepper Vinaigrette

VINAIGRETTE
1/2 cup olive oil

1/4 cup water

3 tablespoons distilled white vinegar

4 teaspoons Dijon mustard

1/2 cup chopped white onion

1/3 cup chopped red bell pepper

1/3 cup chopped yellow bell pepper

1/3 cup chopped orange bell pepper

1/3 cup chopped fresh parsley

3 avocados, peeled, halved, pitted, thinly sliced lengthwise.

1 (14-ounce) can hearts of palm, drained, cut into 1/2 -inch-thick rounds.

Whisk oil, water, vinegar and mustard in a medium bowl. Add onion, all bell peppers, parsley and stir to blend. Season dressing with salt and pepper.

Arrange 1 sliced avocado half, slightly fanned, on each of 6 plates. Divide hearts of palm among plates. Drizzle each serving generously with dressing.

Serves 6

The colors are vibrant in this salad and look beautiful with the avocado and hearts of palm.

5 tablespoons olive oil, divided
6 large romas, cored, halved crosswise, seeded
2 small garlic cloves, thinly sliced
2 tablespoons minced thyme, divided
1 sheet frozen puff pastry, thawed
1 coarsely grated whole milk mozzarella cheese

1/2 cup soft fresh goat cheese (about 4 ounces)
2 large eggs
1/4 cup heavy cream
1/3 cup oil-cured black olives, pitted
2 tablespoons freshly grated Parmesan cheese
8 cups spring greens

Oven-Dried Tomato Tart with Goat Cheese, Black Olives & Spring Greens

Preheat the oven to 300 degrees. Line a rimmed baking sheet with parchment paper; brush with 1 tablespoon oil. Place tomato halves, cut side up, on a baking sheet. Sprinkle garlic and 1 tablespoon thyme over tomatoes; drizzle remaining 1/4 cup oil over. Sprinkle lightly with salt and pepper. Bake until tomatoes begin to shrink and are slightly dried but still soft, about 2 hours. Cool tomatoes on sheet. Can be prepared 1 day ahead. Store in a single layer in covered container in refrigerator.

Roll out pastry. Transfer to a 9-inch diameter tart pan with removable bottom, pressing pastry firmly onto bottom and sides of pan. Trim overhang to 3/4 inch. Fold overhang in and press, pushing crust 1/4 inch above pan. Pierce crust all over with fork; chill 30 minutes.

Preheat the oven to 375 degrees. Line the pastry with foil; fill with pie weights. Bake until crust is set, about 2 minutes. Remove foil and weights; bake until crust edges are golden, piercing with a fork if crust bubbles, about 12 minutes longer. Cool crust 10 minutes. Reduce oven temperature to 350 degrees.

Meanwhile, using a fork, mash mozzarella cheese, goat cheese, and remaining 1 tablespoon thyme together in a medium bowl. Season with salt and pepper. Add eggs and cream and stir until mixture is well blended. Spread cheese filling evenly in crust. Arrange tomato halves in filling, cut side up. Place olives between tomatoes. Sprinkle Parmesan cheese evenly over the top. Bake until filling is puffed and set, about 35 minutes. Cool 5 minutes. Push up pan bottom, releasing sides. Serve tart warm with the spring greens lightly dressed with olive oil and lemon juice.

Serves 8

Oven-dried tomatoes become very sweet. They store well covered with olive oil for future use, great in pasta dishes.

Blue Cheese Coleslaw with Bacon

8 bacon slices, chopped
1/4 cup mayonnaise
2 tablespoons red wine vinegar
1 tablespoon honey
16 ounces purchased coleslaw mix
1 cup crumbled blue cheese

Cook bacon in a large skillet until crisp. Using a slotted spoon, transfer bacon to paper towels.

Whisk mayonnaise, vinegar and honey in a large bowl. Stir in coleslaw mix, cheese and bacon. Season with salt and pepper and toss to coat.

NOTE: Can be made 2 hours ahead. Cover and chill.

Serves 10

Applewood smoked bacon really enhances the flavor of this simple coleslaw.
Adding blue cheese takes it over the top.
Serve with barbecue sirloin or flank steak.

Avocado, Grapefruit & Spring Greens with Citrus Vinaigrette

6 cups spring greens
1 large shallot, diced
2 tablespoons Champagne vinegar
1 tablespoon lemon juice
1 tablespoon orange juice
2 grapefruit, peeled, white pith removed
1/4 teaspoon finely chopped lemon zest
1/4 teaspoon finely chopped orange zest
3/4 cup olive oil
2 avocados, halved, skins left on

Wash and dry the greens. In a medium bowl, combine the shallot with the vinegar, 1 tablespoon each of lemon juice and orange juice, and a pinch of salt.

Cut the grapefruit into sections by slicing along the membranes to free the fruit, reserve.

Whisk the olive oil into the shallot mixture. Add the lemon and orange zests. Add more olive oil if desired.

Cut the avocados into lengthwise slices about the same size as the grapefruit sections. Scoop out the slices with a large spoon. Toss the greens and grapefruit into a large bowl with about two-thirds of the dressing. Taste the salad and add more salt, if necessary. Arrange on a platter. Distribute the avocado slices alongside the salad, season them with salt, and drizzle with the rest of the vinaigrette.

This is a great brunch salad served with scrambled or baked egg dishes

Serves 6

Dressings & Accoutrements

Sweet Basil Vinaigrette

1/2 cup balsamic vinegar
Juice of 1 lime
5 to 7 fresh basil leaves,
cut into thin strips
Salt and freshly ground black pepper
1/2 cup olive oil

Whisk the vinegar, lime juice, basil, salt and pepper together in a small bowl. Slowly add the olive oil, whisking until all the oil is incorporated. Season with additional salt and pepper to taste. Use immediately or refrigerate in an airtight container for up to 1 week.

Smoked Chile Dressing

1/4 cup red wine vinegar
1 clove garlic, coarsely chopped
2 tablespoons chopped red onion
1 tablespoon honey
1 teaspoon salt
3/4 cup canola oil
1 chipotle chile in adobo sauce

Combine the vinegar, garlic, onion, chipotle, honey and salt in a blender and blend until smooth. With the motor running, slowly add the oil and blend until emulsified. This can be made up to 1 day in advance and refrigerated.

Champagne Vinaigrette

1 tablespoon champagne vinegar
1/4 teaspoon salt
3 tablespoons olive oil
Freshly ground pepper

Stir together the champagne vinegar and the salt. Add the olive oil in a slow, steady stream, whisking until emulsified. Season with freshly ground pepper. Sliced melon and prosciutto go well with this vinaigrette.

Lemon-Garlic Vinaigrette

Zest of 1 lemon
Juice of 2 lemons
2 garlic cloves, crushed
1/2 teaspoon salt
1/2 cup olive oil
Freshly ground black pepper

Stir together the lemon zest, juice, garlic and salt. Add the olive oil in a slow steady stream. Season with freshly ground black pepper. Add some fresh oregano and put this vinaigrette on a Greek salad.

Creamy Tarragon Vinaigrette

2 tablespoons tarragon vinegar
1/4 teaspoon Dijon mustard
1/4 cup extra-virgin olive oil
1/4 cup sour cream
2 tablespoons finely
chopped fresh tarragon
Salt and freshly ground black pepper

Stir together the tarragon vinegar and Dijon mustard. Season with coarse salt. Pour in 1/4 cup olive oil in a slow, steady stream, whisking until emulsified. Stir in the sour cream and the tarragon. Season with freshly ground pepper.

This vinaigrette is great for potato salad.

Orange Vinaigrette

1 tablespoon orange zest
3/4 cup orange juice
2 tablespoons sherry vinegar
1/2 teaspoon salt
1/2 cup olive oil
Salt and freshly ground black pepper

Stir together the orange zest, orange juice, sherry vinegar and salt. Add the olive oil in slow, steady stream, whisking until emulsified. Season with salt and pepper.

Try this vinaigrette on sliced beets.

Shallot Vinaigrette

1 shallot, finely chopped
5 oil-packed anchovy fillets, chopped
2 tablespoons red-wine vinegar
1 teaspoon Dijon mustard
1 1/2 teaspoons salt
3/4 cup olive oil
Fresh ground black pepper

Place the shallot, anchovy fillets, red-wine vinegar, mustard and the salt in a blender. With the blender running, pour in the olive oil in a slow, steady stream until emulsified. Season with freshly ground black pepper. Serve this on baby romaine and sliced red onion.

Lime-Chile Dressing

5 tablespoons fresh lime juice
3 tablespoons fresh Asian fish sauce
2 tablespoons rice-wine vinegar
1 tablespoon sugar
1 finely chopped jalapeño
2 garlic cloves, finely minced
2 shallots, thinly sliced
2 tablespoons finely chopped fresh cilantro

Stir together the lime juice, Asian fish sauce, rice-wine vinegar, sugar, jalapeño, garlic and shallots. Stir in the finely chopped cilantro. Shred a rotisserie chicken and add to the dressing. Serve in butter lettuce cups for lunch.

These next few pages aren't salads!
They're just some favorites I wanted you to have fun with.

-Linda

Monkey Bread with Bacon

1/2 pound bacon
2 cans biscuits
1/3 cup melted butter
1/4 cup chopped green,
yellow and red bell pepper
1/4 cup chopped onions
1/4 cup grated Parmesan cheese

Fry the bacon until crisp. Drain and crumble. In the same pan, saute the peppers and onions just until opaque.

Cut the biscuits in quarters.

In a mixing bowl combine all of the ingredients, mixing lightly with a spoon. Pour into a well-greased bundt pan.

Bake 20 minutes at 400 degrees. Pull apart, after inverting onto a serving dish.

Serves 6

Tomato Soup with Goat-Cheese Fondue

1/2 cup olive oil
2 onions, chopped
3 stalks celery, chopped
6 cloves garlic, chopped
3 pounds canned Italian plum tomatoes, peeled and seeded, with liquid
2 quarts chicken stock
2 tablespoons coarse salt
2 tablespoons freshly ground pepper
1 cup chopped fresh basil
4 tablespoons butter

GOAT-CHEESE FONDUE

4 ounces soft goat cheese
1/2 cup heavy cream
2 tablespoons butter
Salt and freshly ground pepper to taste
1/2 teaspoon freshly ground cumin
2 tablespoons chopped chives

For the soup: Heat olive oil in a large saucepan or soup pot. Add onions, celery and garlic. Cook over low heat for 3 minutes, stirring occasionally.

Add all other ingredients, except butter. Cover and simmer over low heat for 2 to 3 hours.

Purée soup in a food processor. Depending on the size of your processor, you may have to do this in 2 or more steps.

Return soup to pot and bring to a simmer. Add butter and whisk until butter is completely blended into soup. Cook for 30 minutes, or until soup has thickened. Correct seasoning.

Pour soup into individual soup bowls and serve with Goat-Cheese Fondue.

For the fondue: Combine cheese and cream in a small saucepan. Bring to a simmer over low heat, whisking to combine. Add butter and whisk together. Season with salt, pepper and cumin, and stir in chives.

NOTE: To give this soup a twist, cut out rounds of puff pastry and make a dome over the bowl. Use a little water to seal the top and cut an air-vent to let out steam. Brush the top with an egg wash and bake at 400 degrees for about 15 minutes or until golden brown.

Serves 10

Baked Chile Onion Rings

3 tablespoons all-purpose flour
1 tablespoon sugar
1 teaspoon chili powder
1 teaspoon ground cumin
1/2 teaspoon salt
1/2 teaspoon paprika
2 large egg whites, slightly beaten
1 pound Vidalia or other
sweet onions, cut into
1/2-inch thick slices and separated into
rings (about 2 large)
1 1/2 cups dry breadcrumbs, divided
Cooking spray

Preheat the oven to 450 degrees

Combine the flour, sugar, chili powder, cumin, salt, paprika and egg whites in a large bowl. Dip onion rings in flour mixture. Place half of the rings in a zip-top plastic bag; add 1/4 cup bread crumbs, shaking bag to coat onion rings. Repeat procedure with remaining onion rings and remaining 3/4 cup breadcrumbs.

Arrange onion rings in a single layer on 2 baking sheets coated with cooking spray. Lightly coat onion rings with cooking spray. Bake at 450 degrees for 5 minutes. Rotate pans on racks; bake 5 minutes. Turn onion rings over, lightly coat with cooking spray and bake 5 minutes. Rotate pans and bake 5 minutes or until crisp. Serve immediately.

Serves 6

SOUP

2 tablespoons olive oil

1 1/2 cups finely chopped yellow onion

Pinch finely ground salt

1 large russet potato, peeled and cut into 1-inch cubes

1 bay leaf

6 cups chicken stock

Salt and freshly ground black pepper

2 pounds asparagus, tough ends removed, cut crosswise into 1/2-inch slices

2 teaspoons finely chopped thyme leaves

2 cups tightly packed fresh spinach leaves

1 cup heavy cream, chilled

2 teaspoons freshly grated lemon zest

PARMIGIANO ZABAGLIONE

2 egg yolks

3 tablespoons dry white wine

Finely ground salt and freshly ground black pepper

1/2 cup grated Parmesan

1/4 cup heavy cream, whipped to soft peaks

Asparagus Soup with Parmigiano Zabaglione

For the soup: Set a large saucepot over high and heat the olive oil. Add the onions, stir briefly, and lower the heat to medium. Add a pinch of salt. Cook the onions until they are soft and translucent but without any browning, about 10 minutes, stirring occasionally. Add the potatoes, bay leaf and chicken stock. Raise the heat to high to bring the stock to a boil, and then lower the heat to simmer. Season with salt and pepper. Cook until the potatoes are tender, about 10 minutes. Add the asparagus and thyme. Return the stock to a simmer. Cook until the asparagus is barely tender.

Remove the bay leaf. Working quickly, ladle some of the soup into a blender with the spinach. Process until the soup is smooth. Add the cream and lemon zest and season with salt and pepper. Keep the soup warm on low heat. If you have an immersion blender this also works well.

For the zabaglione: Bring 2 inches of water to a simmer in a large saucepan. In a large metal bowl, whisk together the egg yolks and wine. Season with salt and pepper. Set the bowl inside the saucepan but not touching the water, and whisk constantly until the mixture has thickened to a point where the whisk can leave a clean trail on the bottom of the bowl, 3 to 5 minutes. Remove the bowl from the heat. Whisk vigorously for 1 minute to cool to room temperature and gradually whisk in the cheese. Season with pepper to taste. Add 1/3 of the whipped cream. Whisk until smooth and then fold in the remaining whipped cream, being careful to keep the mixture light and airy.

To serve, ladle the soup into espresso cups. Spoon the zabaglione over each serving (about 1 teaspoon for each espresso cup of soup). Serve warm or at room temperature.

Serves 6

Guacamole

2 avocados, pitted, chopped
2 cloves grated garlic
(use a microplane for the garlic)
1/2 cup chopped fresh cilantro
2 tablespoons fresh lime juice
1 jalapeño, finely chopped
1 scallion, finely chopped
Salt to taste

Pulse the avocados, garlic, cilantro, lime juice and jalapeño in a food processor until chunky.

Add the salt to taste and garnish with finely chopped scallion.

Goat Cheese & Green Onion Scones

1 cup all-purpose flour
1 cup cake flour
1 tablespoon baking powder
1 teaspoon salt
1/2 teaspoon ground pepper
4 ounces chilled soft mild goat cheese
(such as Montrachet), crumbled
3 large green onions, thinly sliced
3/4 cup chilled half and half
1 large egg

Preheat oven to 375 degrees.

Mix first 4 ingredients in large bowl. Add cheese and green onions and toss with fork. Beat half and half and egg to blend in small bowl. Stir egg mixture into dry ingredients and mix gently until dough forms.

Divide dough in half. On lightly floured surface, flatten each piece into 3/4-inch thick round. Cut each round into 6 wedges. Transfer wedges to baking sheet, spacing evenly.

Bake scones until tops are brown, about 25 minutes. Cool 10 minutes. Serve warm.

NOTE: Scones make great small sandwiches spread with mustard and filled with sliced ham and tomatoes.

Serves 12

AIOLI Garlic mayonnaise from the Provence region of Southern France. Used for salad dressing and for an accompaniment for fish, meat or vegetables.

AL DENTE An Italian phrase meaning "to the tooth," used to describe pasta or other food that is cooked until it offers a slight resistance when bitten into, but is not soft or overdone.

ARUGULA Bitter aromatic green with a peppery, mustard flavor.

ASIAGO A semifirm Italian cheese with a rich, nutty flavor. It is made from whole or part-skim cow's milk.

BALSAMIC Vinegar made from Trebbiano grape juice, it gets its dark color and pungent sweetness from aging in barrels of various woods and in graduating sizes over a period of years.

BOCCONCINI Italian for "mouthful," refers to small balls of mozzarella.

BOSC PEAR A large winter pear with a slender neck and a russeted yellow skin. It is available October through April.

CARAMELIZE When natural sugar is released to form a sweet crust on fruit or vegetables. Caramelizing sugar is to heat it until it liquefies and becomes a clear syrup turning a beautiful caramel color.

CARPACCIO Carpaccio consists of thin shavings of raw beef or vegetables.

CHERVIL A mild flavored member of the parsley family.

CHILE PASTE This paste is made of fermented fava beans, flour, red chiles and sometimes garlic.

CHILE POWDER A powdered seasoning mixture of dried chiles, garlic, oregano, cumin, coriander and cloves.

CHIPOTLE A dried smoked jalapeno. Chipotles can be found dried, pickled and canned in adobo sauce. They are "hot" and smoky.

CLAFOUTI Originally a country French dessert made by topping a layer of fresh fruit with batter. A savory clafouti can be made with vegetables such as tomatoes.

CONFIT Usually refers to preserving meat with salt and slowly cooked in its own fat. It can also refer to a jam or preserve.

COTIJA CHEESE A Mexican cheese that resembles feta. It is not salty but crumbly.

CRÈME FRAÎCHE Made from combining 1 cup of whipping cream and 2 tablespoons buttermilk in a glass container. Cover and let stand 8 to 24 hours. It can also be purchased at your favorite grocery store.

CURRY POWDER Curry powder is a pulverized blend of up to 20 spices, herbs and seeds.

DIJON MUSTARD Originally from Dijon, France, this pale grayish-yellow mustard is known for its clean, sharp flavor.

EDAMAME The Japanese name for green soybeans.

FETA A classic Greek cheese traditionally made of sheep's or goat's milk.

FIG Originally from Southern Europe, Asia and Africa, figs were thought to be sacred and a symbol of peace and prosperity. Most popular the Mission fig, Calimyrna, and Kadota.

GOAT CHEESE Chevre is French for "goat" cheese and is a pure white goat's milk cheese with a tart flavor.

GORGONZOLA Named for a town outside Milan it is a cow's milk cheese rich and creamy with bluish-green veins.

GRUYÈRE Swiss Gruyère a cow's milk cheese has a rich, sweet, nutty flavor.

HAAS AVOCADO A pebbly textured almost black fruit with a buttery texture and milk, faintly nutlike flavor. Eighty percent of today's crop comes from California.

HEIRLOOM Seeds that come in ancient varieties of native non-hybrid plants. Tomatoes are the most popular and found in some specialty produce markets and farmers markets.

HYDROPONIC The science of growing plants in a liquid nutrient solution rather than in soil. The air and light in a hydroponic enclosure is strictly controlled to insure optimal product.

PARSLEY Italian parsley is the more strongly flavored flat-leaf parsley.

EGGPLANT Japanese eggplant is narrow and straight and ranges in color from solid purple to striated shakes and has a tender, slightly sweet flesh.

KALAMATA Kalamata olives are a dark eggplant color and have a rich and fruity flavor.

LEEK Looking like a giant scallion, the leek is related to both the garlic and the onion, though its flavor and fragrance are milder and more subtle.

MÂCHE Native to Europe Mâche has an "alias". It is called corn salad, but has nothing to do with corn. It has dark green leaves that are tender, tangy and have a nutlike flavor in the leaves. Known also as field lettuce and lamb's lettuce.

MANCHEGO Spain's most famous cheese, originally made only from the milk of Manchego sheep that graze on the plains of La Mancha. It has a rich, golden, semi-firm cheese with a full, mellow flavor.

MARJORAM Marjoram is a member of the mint family. It has oval, pale green leaves and a mild, sweet, oregano-like flavor.

MIRIN A low-alcohol, sweet, golden wine made from glutinous rice. Also referred to as rice wine.

MOLASSES During the refining of sugar cane and sugar beets, the juice squeezed from these plants is boiled to a syrupy mixture from which the sugar crystals are extracted. Light molasses comes from the first boiling and is lighter in both flavor and color.

MOZZARELLA (Fresh) Packaged in whey or water. It is generally made from whole milk and has a much softer texture and a sweet, delicate flavor.

NICOISE Olives hailing from Provence n France this small, oval olive ranges in color from purple-brown to brown-black. They are cured in brine and packed in olive oil. They have a rich, nutty, mellow flavor.

OLIVE OIL (Extra Virgin) is the cold-pressed result of the first pressing of the olives, it is only one percent acid. It is the finest and fruitiest of the olive oils.

ORZO Tiny, rice-shaped pasta.

PANCETTA An Italian bacon that is cured with salt and spices but not smoked.

PANKO Breadcrumbs used in Japanese cooking for coating fried foods. They are coarser and create a crunchy crust.

PARMESAN A dry, hard cheese made from skimmed or partially skimmed cow's milk. Aging determines whether it is made in the U.S. or Italy.

PEPPERONCINI Tuscan peppers, two to three inches long, these chiles have a bright red wrinkled skin. They are most often pickled and used as part of an antipasto.

PESTO An uncooked sauce made with fresh basil, garlic, pine nuts, Parmesan and olive oil. "Pestos" can be made from myriad other ingredients such as cilantro to mint.

PIÑON NUTS Spanish for pine nut.

POBLANO CHILE A dark, green chile with a rich flavor that varies from mild to smoky.

POLENTA A staple of Northern Italy it is a mush made from cornmeal.

PROSCIUTTO Ham that has been seasoned, salt-cured (but not smoked) and air-dried.

PUFF PASTRY A delicate, multi-layered pastry made by placing chilled butter between layers of pastry.

RADICCHIO Red-leafed Italian chicory.

RATATOUILLE "An adorable rat?" Or a Provencal dish that combines eggplant, tomatoes, onions, bell peppers, zucchini, garlic and herbs all simmered in olive oil.

SAFFRON Yellow-orange stigmas from a small purple crocus. Each flower provides only 3 stigmas, which must be carefully hand-picked and then dried. Extremely labor intensive and expensive. It takes 14,000 stigmas for each ounce of saffron.

SERRANO A small hot, savory chile used in guacamole and salsa.

SHALLOT An onion-family member formed more like garlic than onions and has the more subtle flavor of both.

SOUFFLÉ A light, airy mixture that begins with a thick egg yolk-based sauce that is lightened by stiffly beaten egg whites. Soufflés may be savory or sweet, hot or cold.

TAPENADE A thick paste made from capers, anchovies, ripe olives, olive oil, lemon juice and seasonings.

WALNUT OIL A nutty-flavored oil extracted from walnut meats. Refrigerate to prevent rancidity.

ZABAGLIONE Traditionally a dessert made by whisking together egg yolks, Marsala wine and sugar. It is done very carefully over simmering water so that the egg yolks cook as they thicken into a light, foamy custard. Leave out the wine, add cheese and serve on top of soup as a savory sauce.

Glossary

Index

Index

Index

Index

www.lindasteidel.com